Praise for *Bible and Breakfast*

Nourish your soul with Asheritah's "delicious" book! These pages will give you practical ways to make much of Him in your mornings—and make healthy meals to kick-start your family's day. A must-have book for every family!

LARA CASEY
Author of *Cultivate* and *Make It Happen*

Every mom needs this book. Deeply nourishing both physically and spiritually, it creates a doable as well as delicious way to start your mornings.

MANDY ARIOTO
President and CEO, MOPS International

If you struggle to make a consistent habit of morning time spent in God's presence, pick this up! The versatility to fit both the days you can only squeeze in a few minutes and those you have a bit longer to meditate make this flexible, so you can stick with it and create that life-giving habit our hearts are desperately longing for.

VALERIE WOERNER
Author of *Grumpy Mom Takes a Holiday* and owner of Val Marie Paper

This is such a fun book! I love the recipes and pictures and the whole idea of it. Asheritah provides recipes for thirty-one different breakfasts and Bible studies to go along with each recipe. It could stand alone as either a Bible study or a cookbook, but the combo is a delight!

BARB RAVELING
Author of *Taste for Truth: A 30-Day Weight Loss Bible Study*

As a busy mom to five blessings, I've often struggled with the discipline of being in God's Word every morning. I wish I had a book like *Bible and Breakfast* when my kids were young, but I'm so glad it's never too late. With a warm and inviting daily welcome to "taste and see that the Lord is good," Asheritah offers us a simple and creative way to feed both our bodies and souls as we spend time with Him. I can't think of a better way to start my morning.

JEN SCHMIDT
Author of *Just Open the Door* and the encourager behind the *Balancing Beauty and Bedlam* blog

After spending thirty-one days with *Bible and Breakfast,* you'll be encouraged to continue meeting with Jesus over breakfast, not out of guilt, but because of the joy of starting your day with Him. *Bible and Breakfast* is the kind of book that will make you want to text your friends to join you in the thirty-one days of meeting with Jesus over breakfast.

KAT LEE
Author of *Hello Mornings* and founder of HelloMornings.org

The Bible is a rich feast, piled high with meaty truth. And yet, as a busy mom with days full of endless tasks, I struggle to find time to dig into God's Word like I want to. I'm so grateful for *Bible and Breakfast* by Asheritah Ciuciu. It brings God's Word right to my breakfast table so I can easily taste and see that the Lord is good.

ERIN DAVIS
Author, blogger, Bible teacher (and a big fan of breakfast)

Bible and Breakfast is a gospel-drenched and biblically-rich devotional that somehow also remains grace-filled and stress-free. As a busy young newlywed, this book was refreshment for my soul and inspiration for my meal plan. *Bible and Breakfast* will provide both spiritual and physical nourishment, and you will find yourself more than satisfied by it.

JAQUELLE CROWE FERRIS
Author of *This Changes Everything: How the Gospel Transforms the Teen Years*

FEEDING
OUR BODIES
AND SOULS
TOGETHER

Bible & breakfast

31 MORNINGS WITH JESUS | Asheritah Ciuciu

MOODY PUBLISHERS
CHICAGO

All Scripture quotations, unless otherwise indicated, are taken from the Holy Bible, New International Version®, NIV®. Copyright © 1973, 1978, 1984, 2011 by Biblica, Inc.™ Used by permission of Zondervan. All rights reserved worldwide. www.zondervan.com. The "NIV" and "New International Version" are trademarks registered in the United States Patent and Trademark Office by Biblica, Inc.™

Scripture quotations marked ESV are from The Holy Bible, English Standard Version® (ESV®), copyright © 2001 by Crossway, a publishing ministry of Good News Publishers. Used by permission. All rights reserved.

Scripture quotations marked MSG are from The Message, copyright © 1993, 2002, 2018 by Eugene H. Peterson. Used by permission of NavPress. All rights reserved. Represented by Tyndale House Publishers, Inc.

All emphasis in Scripture has been added.

Details of some stories have been changed to protect the privacy of individuals. Names and/or details have been modified in the book.

Published in association with Literary Agent Tawny Johnson of D.C. Jacobson and Associates LLC, PO Box 80945, Portland, OR 97280.

Edited by Amanda Cleary Eastep
Author photo: Ashley McComb Productions
Cover and interior design: Erik M. Peterson
Cover and interior photography by Ashley McComb Productions (ashleymccomb.com)

All websites and phone numbers listed herein are accurate at the time of publication but may change in the future or cease to exist. The listing of website references and resources does not imply publisher endorsement of the site's entire contents. Groups and organizations are listed for informational purposes, and listing does not imply publisher endorsement of their activities.

Library of Congress Cataloging-in-Publication Data

Names: Ciuciu, Asheritah, author.
Title: Bible and breakfast : 31 mornings with Jesus--feeding our bodies and
   souls together / Asheritah Ciuciu.
Description: Chicago : Moody Publishers, 2019. | Includes bibliographical
   references. | Summary: "A beautiful book with 31 devotional prompts, 31
   healthy, speedy, and tasty breakfast recipes, and full-color pictures
   from an author you love"-- Provided by publisher.
Identifiers: LCCN 2019022950 (print) | LCCN 2019022951 (ebook) | ISBN
   9780802419354 (hardcover) | ISBN 9780802498137 (ebook)
Subjects: LCSH: Devotional exercises. | Breakfasts. | Cookbooks.
Classification: LCC BV4832.3 .C55 2019 (print) | LCC BV4832.3 (ebook) |
   DDC 242--dc23
LC record available at https://lccn.loc.gov/2019022950
LC ebook record available at https://lccn.loc.gov/2019022951

ISBN: 978-0-8024-1935-4

We hope you enjoy this book from Moody Publishers. Our goal is to provide high-quality, thought-provoking books and products that connect truth to your real needs and challenges. For more information on other books and products written and produced from a biblical perspective, go to www.moodypublishers.com or write to:

Moody Publishers
820 N. LaSalle Boulevard
Chicago, IL 60610

1 3 5 7 9 10 8 6 4 2

Printed in the United States of America

TO CARISSA, AMELIA, AND THEO

YOU TRANSFORMED *BIBLE AND BREAKFAST*
FROM A PERSONAL PRACTICE
INTO A FAMILY TRADITION.

May Jesus' Word and presence be
ever-precious in your lives.

Contents

When they landed, they saw
a fire of burning coals there
with fish on it, and some bread. . . .
Jesus said to them,
"Come and have breakfast."

JOHN 21:9, 12A

Let's Get Started!

Do you feel like you're running on empty? Like you want to read the Bible but just don't have time?

You're not alone.[1] A recent survey revealed that two out of three American women want to read the Bible more than they currently do, but few of us actually grow in our daily Bible reading habits.[2]

I get it. I've been there too.

In 2016, I invited my blog readers to join me in a 31-day challenge I called "Bible and Breakfast." The idea was to help us form a habit of meeting with Jesus in the mornings, opening our Bibles together, and trying out some new breakfast ideas too.

Honestly, I didn't know if anyone would be interested, but I figured it was worth a try, right?

The response was overwhelming. In just a week, more than a thousand women signed up to join me, and for 31 days we swapped recipes and Scripture insights—all from our own kitchen tables around the world. Since that blog series ran a few years ago, I've received countless emails from readers who are still meeting Jesus over breakfast, hopefully forming a lifelong habit from our short time together. So imagine my joy when Moody Publishers offered to collect that series and expand on it for this book you're holding in your hands.

These pages are meant to be scribbled, doodled, and maybe even splattered on as you jot down notes over your morning meals in the weeks to come. I hope you'll encounter Jesus in His Word in a fresh way, and that when you reference this book in the coming years, you'll smile fondly at the records of how God fed you each morning and stirred in your heart a hunger for Him—the beginning of your own lifelong habit of *Bible and Breakfast*.

  Each day, you'll find a recipe for one of my favorite breakfast ideas, a short spiritual "Snack" for those mornings you're in a rush, and an inductive Bible study "FEAST" for when you can linger at the table with God's Word.

Spiritual Snacks and Feasts for Busy Women

If you've tried Bible reading plans before and failed, let me assure you that this time is different.

You don't have to rearrange your schedule for *Bible and Breakfast*—it's meant to fit right into your busy life, because Jesus wants to meet us in our mess. Just look at the women He reached out to in the Bible. The Samaritan woman at the well? Hot mess.[3] The woman who had been bleeding twelve years? Kind of a mess.[4] The two sisters Mary and Martha? Yep, them too.[5] Because really, don't we all struggle in one way or another?

Sure, an Instagram-perfect picture of our Bible with a steaming cup of coffee would be nice, but most days will find us opening our Bibles next to a cold breakfast, half-finished homework, unpaid

bills, and something sticky we have yet to investigate. Don't shrink back, friend. Come to Jesus as you are; He welcomes you with open arms.

On the days you only have time for a quick bite, read the *Snack on the Go*—it's a morsel of Scripture that you can consume quickly and meditate on all day long. If you have more time, sit down to *FEAST at the Table* as I walk you through that same passage of Scripture using inductive Bible study prompts. You can pick the Snack one day and pick the FEAST the next, whatever works for you. One is not better than the other, and no one will be checking your book at the end of the month—this is between you and Jesus.

To help you become consistent in your *Bible and Breakfast* habit, I've also included a check-in at the end of each week. This optional section allows you to reflect on what's going well with your new Bible reading habit and what you'd like to change, so you'll be more likely to stick with it in challenging seasons.

But let me warn you: as you nourish your soul with God's Word, His Bread of Life will both satisfy you and make you hungry for more. Don't be surprised if some days you devour both the Snack and FEAST and other days you struggle to work up a spiritual appetite at all. Take one day at a time, and just open your Bible while you eat breakfast.

No more waiting for the perfect time and place. Today is the day for your new beginning.

Frequently Asked Questions

What if I don't eat breakfast?

Listen, I get it. There are days when I skip a morning meal and just grab a granola bar as I head out the door. Not ideal, but it works in a rush, right? But we have a hard time thinking this way about our spiritual food, as if anything short of an hour-long inductive study is cheating. But just as a nourishing snack is better than starving all morning, so a few minutes with Jesus is better than nothing at all.

Throughout this challenge, I'll invite you to think creatively about how to feed your soul while feeding your body, like listening to a Bible passage while munching on an apple during your commute. And if you don't eat anything until lunchtime? Then join in during your lunch hour.

But what if my toddler chatters in my ear?

Sure, we'd all prefer a few moments of peaceful bliss, but if you're a young mama, your quiet moments are few and far between. And I'm right there with you.

That means *Bible and Breakfast* often finds my preschooler, toddler, and baby at my side. It means I'm cutting up pieces of fruit and wiping up spills while rereading the same few verses out loud over and over again. It means answering questions and breaking up squabbles while silently praying I don't lose my temper and slam shut my Bible. But look close and you'll see the beauty of these moments: we're modeling for our children a hunger for God's Word,[6] and we're imprinting on their little souls dozens, hundreds, and even thousands of mornings spent around the breakfast table with Jesus.[7] Even if we only get one crumb that falls from the Master's table, He can multiply it to feed our souls. And it will be enough.

Then later, perhaps when nap time comes around, we softly shut our bedroom door and read the passage one more time, slowly, thoughtfully, before we fall asleep with our cheek resting on the pages. Hey, even Jesus took naps. We can be like Jesus.

And one more thing—sweet empty nester reading these words, would you prayerfully consider inviting a young mom to join you in reading this book together? You may be surprised how many young women wish they'd have older women pouring into them and their children in this way.

Do I have to change what I eat for breakfast?

Nope! Not at all. I want to make it easier for you to make a habit of meeting with Jesus in the morning. If making a new-to-you breakfast gets in the way of that, then by all means stick with your tried-and-true favorites. But if you enjoy culinary adventures, the daily recipes will give you something yummy and nutritious to look forward to.

Are you providing a reading plan?

Yep! You can find a printable reading plan and more helpful bonuses at bibleandbreakfast.com.

Where can I find other women who are reading this book?

Little groups are popping up all over the country, and you can start one in your own neighborhood! You can also find other readers using our hashtag #bibleandbreakfast on social media. Snap a selfie with your copy of this book so we can find and encourage each other as we go!

Can I invite my friends to join too?

Absolutely! In fact, I encourage you to invite a neighbor, sister, or friend to join you in this 31-day adventure. You'll find invitation postcards and shareable graphics for your social media, and other fun bonuses on my book website at bibleandbreakfast.com. And if you're going through this book with a small group, look for the leader's guide and discussion questions while you're there too.

Visit **bibleandbreakfast.com** *to get:*

- a printable reading plan, leader's guide, and discussion questions
- invitation postcards for friends
- shareable social media graphics
- morning worship playlist
- extra book bonuses

On social media? Post a selfie with your book and encourage others! **#bibleandbreakfast**

What if this takes me longer than 31 days, or what if I want to skip around to a different day or a favorite recipe?

Listen, friend, there's no Quiet Time police that will come knocking on your door. While many of us may have grown up with Sunday school teachers who quizzed us on verses and double-checked our worksheets, that's a thing of the past.

This journey is between you and Jesus. Take as much time as you need. Skip around as you'd like. Linger for several days on one passage or feast on multiple passages all at once. Live on the wild side and eat breakfast for dinner with your evening devotions if you're more of a night owl than a morning bird. There is no one-size-fits-all Quiet Time formula in the Bible because God made each of us one-of-a-kind. God is after our hearts, not our checklists. So shed the guilt and accept Jesus' invitation to delight in Him:

> *"Come to me, all you who are weary and burdened, and I will give you rest. Take my yoke upon you and learn from me, for I am gentle and humble in heart, and you will find rest for your souls." (Matt. 11:28–29)*

Rest. Freedom. Joy.

They're all ours when we make our way to Jesus. So grab your Bible, a pen, and an apron, and let's get started.

The Inside Scoop on Bible and Breakfast Recipes

Have you tried to eat "clean" but feel like veggies just don't taste as good as your usual carb-and-sugar-loaded breakfasts?

Or maybe you've tried to serve your family healthy meals but encounter mutiny at the breakfast table.

I get it. I've been there too as I've led my family into a whole-foods lifestyle. So here's my promise to you: I promise to only include my family's favorite recipes that are healthy, yummy, and quick to make.

When I say healthy, I mean breakfasts that incorporate lots of colorful fruits and veggies, good fats, whole grains, plenty of protein, and natural sugars. Yes, sometimes I've allowed for some all-purpose flour or raw sugar instead of completely replacing it with "healthified" versions, but that's because I'm committed to only including recipes my active husband and kids will actually eat. Feel free to adjust to your own family's preferences.

And let's be honest—few of us have time to make breakfast from scratch each morning. So where possible, I've included time-saving tips on meal prepping and freezer cooking. Sometimes I'll meal prep several recipes on the weekend, so I can finish it in a few minutes in the mornings. Other times

I'll double recipes and stash grab-and-go breakfasts in the freezer for busy mornings. You'll see icons indicating both meal prep recipes and freezer-friendly recipes to help you plan ahead.

❄ *Freezer-friendly*

⊘ *Gluten-free*

✋ *Kid-friendly*

☑ *Meal Prep*

Even though I've included breakfast recipes between each of the daily Snack and FEAST devotional prompts, I have ZERO expectations that you'll make a new breakfast recipe each day. I don't. Feel free to earmark the ones you want to try first and leave the others for later. Or invite your friends to join you in a weekly *Bible and Breakfast* club where you each make a recipe and come together to enjoy. That sounds like my kind of party.

I've also noted recipes that are easy to make with kids, because that's my life. At the time of this writing, the ages of my three children range between ten months and five years, and I'm trying to involve them in the cooking process as much as possible. Even though it takes longer this way, they're more likely to eat the food they make, and they're learning important kitchen skills and healthful eating habits. (I know you know this—but please use caution when children are around knives, fire, and other kitchen dangers. And when they spill flour or drop eggs, take a deep breath and laugh it off—it's all part of the experience, and you're making fun memories together.)

As you cook your way through this book, whether alone or with others, I hope you'll not only discover new breakfast favorites but also develop a deeper appreciation for the God who invented food and taste buds. After all, good food was God's idea in the first place, and eating healthfully and joyfully is a wonderful act of worship.

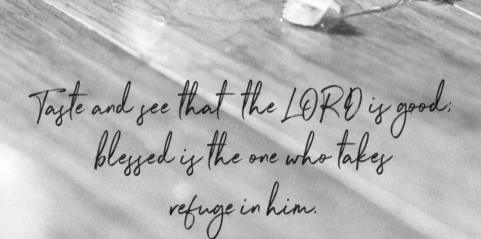

Taste and see that the LORD is good;
blessed is the one who takes
refuge in him.

PSALM 34:8

❄ *Freezer-friendly*

✋ *Kid-friendly*

☑ *Meal Prep*

---

²/₃ cup all-purpose flour

²/₃ cup whole wheat pastry flour

¹/₂ cup cocoa powder

1 tsp baking soda

¹/₂ tsp kosher salt

1 tsp instant coffee, optional

3 ripe bananas, mashed

¹/₄ cup maple syrup

1 tsp vanilla extract

¹/₃ cup Greek yogurt

¹/₃ cup coconut oil, melted

1 large egg, beaten

¹/₃ cup mini chocolate chips,
    plus more for topping

1. Preheat oven to 375 ° F. Spray a 12-cup muffin tin with nonstick cooking spray or line with baking cups.

2. In a large bowl, stir the dry ingredients together (except for the chocolate chips). Use a spatula to gently push the dry ingredients against the sides of the bowl to make a well.

3. In a small bowl, mix together wet ingredients just until combined. Pour wet ingredients into the well and mix carefully, running the spatula around the edge of the bowl and pulling dry ingredients over and into the wet ingredients until barely combined. Some lumps are okay. (This method of mixing ensures your muffins turn out tender.) Gently fold in chocolate chips.

4. Divide batter equally among muffin cups, topping each with a few extra chocolate chips.

5. Bake for 15–17 minutes or until a toothpick inserted into the center comes out clean. Cool on a wire rack. To freeze, wrap cooled muffins in plastic wrap. Store in freezer in an airtight container up to 3 months.

Double Chocolate Banana Muffins

While trying to decide which recipe to feature first in this book, I realized this one was simply begging to go first. Chocolaty, banana-y, yummy, and healthy—it's all I could ask for in a morning muffin, satisfying my sweet tooth while avoiding a sugar crash. You can top these with an extra dollop of Greek yogurt or peanut butter to keep you fueled all morning long.

DAY 1
Start Fresh

 Snack on the go | *If you're in a rush, the short devotional below is a quick "spiritual snack" to feed your soul and meditate on all day long.*

When you think of your grandmother's house, what tastes come to mind?

I can picture Buna, my paternal Romanian grandmother, bent over the stove in her country kitchen, flipping little pastries in a pot of hot oil. The powdered sugar melted as I bit into the puff of airy deliciousness—the memory so vivid I can almost taste it now. And this is good! After all, both food and taste buds are God's gifts to us, and He also gifted us with complex taste-memory neurological pathways that inform our decisions.[8]

When we recall a pleasant food experience, we're more likely to try that same food again. This makes total sense when thinking of Buna's pastries, but it also makes the psalmist's invitation fascinating:

> Taste and see that the LORD is good;
> blessed is the one who takes refuge in him. (Ps. 34:8)

When we personally taste the Lord's goodness, we're creating a pathway in our souls that imprints the memory deep within us and guides us to keep coming back to Him. Elsewhere in Scripture we read that God's Word is as sweet as honey (Ps. 19:10 and 119:103), and Jesus said that He Himself is the bread from heaven that gives life to the world, and "whoever eats this bread will live forever" (John 6:51). In 1 Peter 2:2–3 we're encouraged to continue craving the pure and sweet Word of God since we have already tasted the kindness of the Lord.

Think of it: God's Word could have been compared to a bitter medicine—horrible to swallow but ultimately necessary for our good. Instead, the Lord made Scripture and time with Jesus not only spiritually nourishing but also satisfyingly sweet! And as we feast, we're teaching our souls to keep coming back for more.

If you haven't yet experienced the sweetness of God's Word, well friend, you are in for a treat. Today the Lord is inviting you to taste His goodness and delight your soul in Him. Like children in their grandma's kitchen, let us relish the simple pleasures of His Word.

Read the psalmist's words above again (Ps. 34:8) and rewrite them in your own words as a personal invitation.

Taste and see for yourself that the Lord is good. And then keep coming back each day for more of Him.

 Feast at the table | *If you have more time to linger at the breakfast table, open your Bible and let's FEAST on God's Word together!*

Focus on God

Open your Bible to Matthew 4:4. Write it out as a prayer to the Lord as you begin your study of His Word today.

Engage the Text

Read Psalm 34 out loud. Now, read it again, underlining anything that stands out to you.

Your Bible may contain a description at the very beginning of the psalm, explaining that David wrote these verses when he pretended to be crazy in front of Abimelek. That sounds like a fascinating story! To better understand the context of this psalm, let's back up to 1 Samuel 21:10–15 (where the king is likely being referred to by his name, Achish, rather than a title) and read what happened there. After you read that text, summarize the story below, describing the various threats to David's life.

Let's go back to Psalm 34 now, and read it again. In light of what was going on in David's life at the time, does anything new stand out to you?

Consider the following questions:

How did God show His goodness to David, according to verses 4 and 6–7?

How did David respond to God's goodness (see verses 1–2)?

How does David describe the Lord?

Two of the main themes in this psalm are the Lord's provision and the Lord's deliverance. According to verses 9–10, how does God provide for His people?

How does this psalm describe the Lord's deliverance (see verses 17–20)?

What does David call the righteous to do in verses 3 and 8?

Verse 8 uses taste to describe one's personal experience of God. How did David taste God's goodness? How does he contrast hunger and fullness in verse 10?

According to verses 15–22, how are the righteous and the unrighteous similar? How are they different?

Assess the Main Idea

Summarize the main idea of this psalm in a single sentence.

Spark Transformation

In your own life, what do you need deliverance from? What do you need provision for?

What would it look like for you to "taste and see that the Lord is good" in these areas of your life? In contrast, what does it look like for you to trust yourself?

Turn to God in Worship

In your own life, how can you attest to God's deliverance and goodness? In the space below, recount one specific situation in which God intervened for your good.

Now, as verse 3 says, let's "glorify" Him and "exalt his name." Write a prayer praising the Lord for the ways that He is showing His goodness to you, and trusting Him for the specific situations in your life you've listed above.

PREP TIME: *10 minutes*	COOK TIME: *3 minutes each*	YIELD: *four servings*

❄ *Freezer-friendly*
⊘ *Gluten-free*
✋ *Kid-friendly*
☑ *Meal Prep*

---

4 pint-sized mason jars with lids

Nonstick cooking spray

1 cup shredded sharp Cheddar cheese

1 cup diced ham

1 cup finely chopped onion

1 red pepper, finely chopped

3 green onions, finely chopped

Salt and pepper, to taste

8 large eggs

Extra shredded cheese and chopped green onions, for serving

1. Spray the inside of the mason jars with nonstick cooking spray. Then layer the ingredients in the mason jars and season with salt and pepper to taste. To freeze, stop at step 1 and screw on the lids. When you're ready to make a fresh omelet, remove the lid and microwave the filling for about one minute. Proceed to step 2.

2. Crack two eggs into each jar. Marvel at the beauty of mason jar breakfasts and snap a picture to share on social media with #bibleandbreakfast.

3. Screw the lids on the jars and give it a few good shakes until the eggs are scrambled and the fillings are all mixed up. Kids especially love doing this part.

4. Remove the lids. This is important! No metal in the microwave, please, unless you want to see a fireworks show. Ask me how I know.

5. Microwave each on high for 2–3 minutes, stirring every 30 seconds. Use an oven mitt when removing because these little jars are hot!! Garnish with extra cheese and green onions.

Mason Jar Omelets

This is the perfect *Bible and Breakfast* on the go . . . I prep one of these as I'm getting the kids out the door and grab bites at stoplights while we listen to the audio Bible. This recipe easily doubles or triples if you're meal prepping for the month, and it's infinitely customizable with your favorite omelet fillings.

DAY 2
Made Right

 **Snack on the go** | *If you're in a rush, the short devotional below is a quick "spiritual snack" to feed your soul and meditate on all day long.*

Why did Jesus die?

That may seem like a simple question, especially if you've spent much time in church, but take a moment to really consider your answer.

Why did Jesus die?

These are the kinds of questions my preschooler asks me, and I try to give her age-appropriate answers that teach her who God is. But every time she asks a question I'm challenged to rethink the answer for myself.

Why *did* Jesus die? And what would have happened had He not died?

If I spent the rest of my days trying to understand the magnitude of what happened on the cross, I would still only scratch the surface.[9] But recently God has been teaching me one reality of what happened on the cross through my study in Galatians 2:21: "I do not set aside the grace of God, for if righteousness could be gained through the law, Christ died for nothing!"

Wow. Those are strong words! To think that Christ could have died for nothing ought to give us pause. But Paul argues that if we rely on our own good works (law) to secure God's forgiveness and favor (righteousness), then we're basically rejecting Christ's death on the cross (as good for nothing).

None of our works are good enough to secure God's favor. But the good news is that we can stop trying to impress God and rest instead in Jesus' finished work on the cross. He lived the perfect life, died a sinner's death, and was resurrected to victorious life to invite us to join His royal family forever and ever.

Why did Jesus die? That's one reason why. As you reflect on this invitation, what's one thing you want to say to Jesus in response?

If you haven't yet received God's gift of forgiveness in Jesus, make today the day. Admit that your own good works are not good enough to save you. Believe that Jesus died for your sins and was raised to life again. Confess to God that you need His forgiveness. Open wide your hands to receive His gift of life with Him forever as His beloved child. And then share your decision with someone who is a child of God that you may celebrate together!

Feast at the table

If you have more time to linger at the breakfast table, open your Bible and let's FEAST on God's Word together!

Focus on God

Open your Bible to 1 Peter 2:2, and ask God to grow your appetite for His Word.

Engage the Text

Read Galatians 2:11–21 out loud. In your own words, describe the confrontation between Paul and Peter. Why was Paul upset with Peter?

Read Acts 11:1–18 for more context. How did Peter's vision affect his understanding of Old Testament prohibitions regarding clean and unclean foods?

What were the implications for non-Jewish converts (see Acts 11:18)? In other words, how would Peter's vision affect them?

In light of this context, why did Paul react so strongly to Peter's actions described in Galatians 2?

At issue here is the question of how a person is made right with God. According to verse 16, what is Paul's answer?

How does human effort to gain favor with God downplay Jesus' sacrifice on the cross (Gal. 2:21b)?

The climax of Paul's argument is found in verses 20–21. Rewrite these verses in your own words.

Assess the Main Idea

In one sentence, summarize the main point of this passage.

Spark Transformation

This temptation to seek God's favor through our behavior continues to be a struggle for twenty-first-century believers. What does this look like in your life? How are you tempted to allow old rules to steal the glory of Jesus' sacrifice?

Turn to God in Worship

Today, take a few moments to express to God your need to understand His grace in a new and deeper way. Ask God to show you any ways you're trying to earn His love, and then worship Jesus for His finished work on the cross.

❄ *Freezer-friendly*

⊘ *Gluten-free*

☑ *Meal Prep*

---

8 cups water

1 tsp salt

2 cups yellow polenta (although I usually use cornmeal because that's what I have on hand)

1/4 tsp freshly ground black pepper

4 oz sharp Cheddar cheese, freshly grated, plus additional for topping, if desired

4 oz Parmesan cheese, freshly grated

3 large eggs, beaten

1 cup whole milk

12 oz breakfast sausage

1. Preheat oven to 350° F.

2. In a large saucepan, bring to a boil the water and salt. In a separate pan, cook the sausage (breaking it up into pieces) until it's no longer pink, then set aside.

3. Using a wire whisk, stir the water to create a vortex, and slowly add polenta, stirring continuously. Slow and steady here—adding too much too soon will result in clumps, but a steady stream will give you a smooth composition. Cover, reduce heat to low, and cook for 10 minutes. Stir frequently to avoid sticking.

4. Add pepper and cheeses, stirring until melted. Remove from heat and stir in eggs and milk until combined.

5. Pour half the polenta into an 8x11 greased baking dish. Layer in the breakfast sausage, then top with remaining polenta. Bake about an hour until set and lightly browned. Top with additional cheese and broil until cheese forms a crunchy layer. Let cool 15 minutes before serving.

Optional: Double the recipe, and freeze the unbaked extra portion in a baking dish for up to 3 months. To bake, thaw overnight in the fridge, and then allow the dish to warm up on the stove top while you preheat the oven. Increase the total baking time from one hour to about 90 minutes.

Baked Cheesy Polenta

This reminds me of my childhood in Romania, where polenta is a kitchen staple and readily served for breakfast, lunch, or dinner. But the addition of cheese, eggs, and sausage transforms this from a side dish into a protein-packed breakfast. Plus you can prep everything the night before and just pop it in the oven in the morning to bake while you dig into God's Word. Pair with a side of fresh fruit salad (p. 45) and you have yourself a complete breakfast.

DAY 3
Trusting the Provider

 Snack on the go | *If you're in a rush, the short devotional below is a quick "spiritual snack" to feed your soul and meditate on all day long.*

"No, it's not!" my preschooler protests.

"Yes, sweetie," I counter, trying to keep my voice even. "This is the way to Grandma's house."

"No, it's not!" comes her retort.

She had been challenging me on the smallest details of our routine until one day she quietly asked, "How do you know SO MANY THINGS?" I realized her challenges were born not out of defiance, but out of wonder. Within her small understanding of the world, my own limited knowledge seemed gargantuan—so far beyond her comprehension that the only way to process it was to doubt.

Don't we often do the same with God? From where we're standing, arms crossed in defiance, we can't see God working disjointed details for our good and His glory (Rom. 8:28–30). Yet God's thoughts are far beyond our thoughts, as high as the heavens are from the earth (Isa. 55:8–9).

Like little children, we doubt what we don't know. But the Bible is filled with stories of people commended for their faith not because they never doubted, but because they trusted God with their unease. Just look at Hebrews 11 and you'll see that God's people weren't faultless in their faith—they were devoted when details didn't make sense, and they kept seeking Him: "And without faith it is impossible to please God, because anyone who comes to him must believe that he exists and that he rewards those who earnestly seek him" (Heb. 11:6).

God doesn't expect us to understand what He is doing; He invites us to step into a closer walk with Him. This hand-in-hand walk is far different from the cross-armed stance we often start with.

Just as my daughter is learning to trust me, so we learn to trust God—walking with Him as He works in our lives and recognizing His worth in Scripture.

Go for a walk today, bringing to mind the situation in your life that may be causing you to doubt God's goodness and power. Picture yourself taking a hold of your heavenly Father's hand, and declare your trust in Him as you learn to "walk by faith, not by sight" (2 Cor. 5:7 ESV).

 *Feast at the table* | *If you have more time to linger at the breakfast table, open your Bible and let's FEAST on God's Word together!*

Focus on God

Open your Bible to Psalm 33:4. Begin today's study by asking God's Holy Spirit to help you receive what He has to say to you today.

Engage the text

Read Hebrews 11 out loud. In the space below, write a short description of how each of the men and women listed demonstrated faith:

Abel (v. 4):

Enoch (v. 5):

Noah (v. 7):

Abraham (vv. 8–12, 17–19):

Sarah (v. 11):

Isaac (v. 20):

Jacob (v. 21):

Joseph (v. 22):

Moses's parents (v. 23):

Moses (vv. 24–28):

Israelites (v. 29):

Rahab (v. 31):

Gideon, Barak, Samson, Jephthah, David, Samuel, and the prophets (vv. 32–38):

What do these men and women have in common? How are they different?

According to verses 1–2, what is faith?

Why is faith required, according to verse 6?

Choose one of the people mentioned above, and in 2–3 sentences, describe how they demonstrated certainty in what they didn't see. Consider looking up cross-references to read more about their lives.

Throughout history women and men have risked (and sometimes given up) their lives for the sake of their faith in God. And at the time the book of Hebrews was written, the recipients would have been facing persecution for their faith in Jesus at the hands of both Jews and Romans. What assurance does this chapter give regarding the life of faith? In other words, what is the greatest reward of the life of faith, according to verse 6?

What does Jesus say about faith and persecution in Matthew 5:11–12?

As inspiring as it is to reflect on the lives of the faithful in the past, we should not get stuck staring into the rearview mirror. Read Hebrews 12:1–3. The word "therefore" means that everything written in chapter 11 is building up to the culmination that follows. What does the writer instruct his readers to do in these verses?

How is Jesus the ultimate example of a life of faith in God's faithfulness?

Assess the Main Idea

Summarize the main point of Hebrews chapter 11 through 12:3 in a single sentence.

Spark Transformation

Today, take a few moments to do what the writer of Hebrews instructs: confess any sin that is hindering you.

Renew your commitment to live a faith-filled life as you await Jesus' return. Worship Jesus.

Turn to God in worship

What's one attribute of God revealed in today's text that you can praise Him for? Take a few moments to do just that.

As you go about your day, also pray for our sisters and brothers around the world who face persecution for their faith. Want to learn more about the persecuted church today? Check out Voice of the Martyrs at persecution.com.

❄ *Freezer-friendly*

✋ *Kid-friendly*

☑ *Meal Prep*

---

1 cup all-purpose flour

1 cup whole wheat flour

1 cup oat flour

$\frac{1}{2}$ cup quick-cooking oats

$\frac{1}{4}$ cup raw sugar

1 Tbsp baking powder

1 tsp baking soda

$\frac{1}{2}$ tsp salt

$3\frac{1}{2}$ cups buttermilk

2 large eggs

$\frac{1}{3}$ cup coconut oil, melted

1 tsp vanilla extract

1 tsp grated orange zest, optional

1 cup mini chocolate chips, plus more for topping

1. In a large bowl, stir together dry ingredients. Make a well in the center and stir in wet ingredients and the orange zest, if using. This will seem like a lot, but you're stocking up your freezer for busy mornings, so put on some fun music and let's get cooking!

2. Allow the batter to rest for 5 minutes while you clean up the kitchen.

3. Pour a scant $\frac{1}{4}$ cup batter onto a lightly greased griddle, preheated to medium high. Sprinkle a few chocolate chips on top and cook until firm around the edges and bubbles no longer form, about 2 to 4 minutes.

4. Flip and cook until golden brown, about 2 minutes. Be careful—chocolate burns easily, so don't go too far away from the stove. These will probably disappear as soon as you plate them, but if you're trying to keep them warm, stack on a cookie sheet in an oven heated to 175° F.

5. Serve plain or with a small drizzle of maple syrup. My kids also like spreading on strawberry jam and eating them like crepes. Because chocolate and strawberry—why not?

Freezer Oatmeal Chocolate Chip Pancakes

Let's face it: most kids dream of eating pancakes for breakfast every day, while moms cringe at the nutritional disaster pancakes can be. These oatmeal pancakes save the day, balancing whole grains with just enough chocolate to make them delicious naked—no syrup required. This recipe yields enough extras to freeze then microwave on busy mornings.

DAY 4
Filled with Joy

 Snack on the go | *If you're in a rush, the short devotional below is a quick "spiritual snack" to feed your soul and meditate on all day long.*

Have you ever listened to a song that completely brightened your day?

We've long known that music affects our mood, but recent studies suggest it can also change our perception of the world around us. People who listened to happy music were more likely to see happy smiley faces even when there were none. Simply put, what fills our minds will fill our lives.[10]

I've experienced this myself. As a missionary kid, I spent hundreds of hours listening to Bible verses set to music in the car while the landscape rolled by. The upbeat tune made the rides more enjoyable, and to this day, those melodies from long ago come to mind as I read my Bible, and I'm left humming them all day long.

Philippians 4:4 is one of those verses set to song I memorized: "Rejoice in the Lord always. I will say it again: Rejoice!"

Paul repeats himself, emphasizing his desire that the Philippians be filled with joy in Jesus. Such a simple concept, but doesn't it seem so hard? How exactly do we do that?

Perhaps one way is through music. In another letter, Paul instructs believers to "be filled with the Spirit, speaking to one another with psalms, hymns, and songs from the Spirit. Sing and make music from your heart to the Lord" (Eph. 5:18b–19). And this isn't just the New Testament either: the psalms are also filled with calls to sing joyfully to the Lord (see Psalms 33:1–3; 66:1–2; 98:4–5; 149:2–3).

We're not talking about fake positivity, listening to upbeat music while ignoring the hardships in our lives. Quite the opposite. As believers, we cling to the gospel amid our brokenness, singing songs that remind us of who King Jesus is, His victory over sin and death, and His promise to return and bring His kingdom here on earth. Those truths change our perception like nothing else will, causing us to rejoice in the Lord even on the hardest days.

What kind of music fills your life? Does it point you to King Jesus or to empty promises? How might you more intentionally choose songs that help you rejoice in the Lord?

If you're musical, consider making up a little tune for Philippians 4:4, and sing it to yourself today. Or just look up the kid's version online. Let the sticky song make this message stick to your soul and remind you to rejoice even when the kids are cranky, the laundry mounds topple over, and dinner consists of peanut butter and jelly sandwiches. We can rejoice. In Jesus.

Create a playlist of your favorite songs that point you to Jesus and cause you to rejoice in Him and listen only to that music for a month to see how your life changes. Or go to bibleandbreakfast.com to access a playlist of songs I curated just for you!

 Feast at the table | *If you have more time to linger at the breakfast table, open your Bible and let's FEAST on God's Word together!*

Focus on God

Open your Bible to Proverbs 30:5. Turn the verse into a prayer as you begin today's study.

Engage the Text

Read Philippians 4:4–9 out loud.

Now read the text again, more slowly this time, writing down any immediate observations.

In these six verses, Paul gives the Philippians six directives in rapid-fire succession. What are they? List them in the space below.

How are all these directives connected to each other? In other words, what does rejoicing have to do with not worrying and with what we think about?

Let's look at verse 6 more closely. What two forces are described as being in opposition?

How does each affect our own spiritual lives and our testimony to the onlooking world?

What specific instructions does Paul give regarding the way we pray?

In your experience, what is the result of worry? What does it accomplish?

According to verse 7, what is the result of prayer, as Paul describes it here? How does prayer change things?

Assess the Main Idea

In one sentence, write down the main point of this passage.

Spark Transformation

How can you apply today's teaching to your own life? Choose one small and specific way to apply today's main idea in the next 24–48 hours.

Turn to God

Download your very own FEAST bookmark to keep in your Bible or workbook! bibleandbreakfast.com

Picture yourself carrying a heavy backpack filled with all your worries and concerns. As you approach the throne of grace, kneel before the Father (you may actually get on your knees, if you'd like) and take off your backpack. Now, one by one, remove each worry and place it at God's feet. Name it specifically, describe the situation, and give it over to God. Then pause and allow God's peace to flow over you. Imagine it flowing like a river, springing from God's throne and washing over your head, your heart, your hands, all the way to your feet. Rest in God's presence for a few minutes before you go on with your day.

PREP TIME: *10 minutes* | **YIELD:** *7 servings*

⊘ *Gluten-free*

✋ *Kid-friendly*

☑ *Meal Prep*

---

1 lb fresh strawberries, quartered

12 oz fresh blueberries or
 blackberries

12 oz red grapes, halved

4 kiwis, peeled and sliced

2 mangoes, chopped

1 cup pineapple, cut in chunks

2 bananas, sliced

Mint, optional

1. Peeling, chopping, and slicing is the hardest part. (Which is to say, this recipe is a cinch!)

2. Assemble the fruit in a glass bowl, either layering by colors of the rainbow or tossing them all together. The key is to mix in as many colors as possible. Try raspberries, plums, grapefruit, apples, mandarins, cantaloupe, honeydew, and watermelon. Serve with a garnish of mint.

Optional: You can make this fruit salad up to 24 hours ahead of time. If using apples, toss them in lemon juice to keep them from turning brown.

Rainbow
Fruit Salad

When I was a new bride, I wanted to come up with a signature dish that would be my go-to option for potlucks and family gatherings. This fruit salad is the perfect fit, and I've brought it to countless baby showers and birthday parties over the years. Nowadays my preschooler and toddler help wash and layer the fruit, so we often have this sweet side dish for a weekend family brunch.

DAY 5
Real Fruit

 *Snack on the go*

Some days, I sleep in instead of waking to pray. I stare down the driver who stole my parking spot, and I drown my frustrations in a mocha and cake pops. And it's only 9 a.m.

Do you ever have those kinds of mornings?

On those days, I want to crawl into a closet and cry myself to sleep. I'm too ashamed to face Jesus because I feel like I've failed Him when I read: "Whoever wants to be my disciple must deny themselves and take up their cross daily and follow me" (Luke 9:23).

For a long time, I thought this verse meant that I had to clean myself up before coming to Jesus. I had to muster more discipline, more patience, more love, more self-control. I had to hoist my daily burdens onto my shoulders as I trudged after Jesus.

But that's reading this passage through a legalistic try-harder lens, which is contrary to gospel truth. When we read Scripture this way, we're quick to isolate ourselves in our shame and guilt, staying far from Jesus—which is exactly where our enemy wants us.

Let's look at this verse in a different translation, so we can hear it with fresh ears: "Anyone who intends to come with me has to let me lead. You're not in the driver's seat—I am. Don't run from suffering; embrace it. Follow me and I'll show you how. Self-help is no help at all" (MSG).

Jesus doesn't send us away to pull ourselves together; He invites us to let Him lead us through the hard moments. It is His Spirit in us who produces the fruit we're after—love, joy, peace, patience, and so on (Gal. 5:22–23). We can try to muster these virtues on our own, but they're like plastic fruit—lovely on the outside, but hollow on the inside.

When we surrender to Jesus and allow Him to lead, He bears fruit in us (see John 15:4–6), not only transforming our life but drawing others to Himself through our transformation.

This fruitful surrender happens daily. So if you messed up yesterday, take heart. Today is a new day. And if your day has already started off wrong, turn to Jesus and whisper, "I can't do this on my own. I need You. Change my heart and produce Your fruit in me."

That's a prayer He will gladly answer.

 *Feast at the table* | *If you have more time to linger at the breakfast table, open your Bible and let's FEAST on God's Word together!*

Focus on God

Open your Bible to James 1:21. Write out a prayer asking God to till up the soil of your heart and remove any sin so that His Word would fall on fertile ground and bear much fruit.

Engage the Text

Read Luke 9:23–26 out loud. Now read it again, writing down any observations that immediately stand out to you.

According to Jesus, what is required of a disciple?

Becoming a disciple requires an initial commitment to follow the teacher. But how does the word "daily" in verse 23 affect the ongoing nature of this relationship?

What do you make of Jesus' words in verse 24? How is kingdom living the opposite of earthly calculations and projections?

How does the contrast in verse 25 highlight the value of one's eternal destiny in relation to God?

What does verse 26 say about the long-term ramifications of one's decision to reject or be ashamed of Jesus?

Read the passage again. Does anything new stand out to you?

Assess the Main Idea

In verse 25, Jesus talks about gaining the whole world. What does this mean?

Summarize the main idea of this text in a single sentence.

Spark Transformation

What do you want most in life? What would be some of the most valuable accomplishments for a person in your situation?

According to our text today, all these earthly achievements pale in comparison to knowing Jesus personally. Do you believe that to be true in your own life? If you did, how might that influence your priorities today?

What might this daily surrender look like in your own life?

Turn to God in Worship

What does this passage say about God? What do we learn about His character? His worth?

Write a prayer in the space below, praising God for those things that you discovered in today's text, and surrendering yourself to Him anew.

PREP TIME: *3 minutes*	**COOK TIME:** *none*	**YIELD:** *4 servings*

⊘ *Gluten-free*

✋ *Kid-friendly*

☑ *Meal Prep*

———————

2 cups fresh spinach

2 cups water

1 cup fresh or frozen mango,
   chopped

1 cup fresh or frozen pineapple,
   chopped

2 bananas

1 cup Greek yogurt, optional

1. In a high-powered blender, blend spinach and water until liquefied, about 30 to 45 seconds.

2. Add remaining ingredients and blend again. The Greek yogurt is optional but will make your smoothie creamier and pack a protein punch to keep you full longer.

3. Pour into four glasses and enjoy!

To cut down on prep time and cleanup, assemble the fruit and spinach in the jars ahead of time and store in the fridge or freezer. Then blend the fruit and spinach with the other ingredients and pour back into the jars to enjoy!

Beginner's Blessing Green Smoothie

The very first time I tried a green smoothie, it was straight up kale and water and trust me—it was disgusting. I distrusted anything green for a few years until I tried this combo and my life has changed completely, and now even my kiddos will drink green smoothies without even thinking it's a weird thing for kids. The secret is to start with a mild green, like spinach, and throw in sweet fruits like banana and pineapple. And as my five-year-old daughter would say: BOOM! You've been introduced to the gateway green smoothie that will change your life.

DAY 6
Compelled to Bless

 Snack on the go | *If you're in a rush, the short devotional below is a quick "spiritual snack" to feed your soul and meditate on all day long.*

Once is enough.

It only takes a single broken promise to shatter trust.

No matter how much we love someone, in our fallen human nature, people will disappoint us. And we will disappoint them. As you think back on your life, what disappointments come first to mind?

Failures are a normal part of human relationships, and part of maturing means learning to forgive each other. But God is not us. In fact, the Bible says:

> *"God is not human, that he should lie,*
> *not a human being, that he should change his mind.*
> *Does he speak and then not act?*
> *Does he promise and not fulfill?" (Num. 23:19)*

No matter the hurts we've experienced from others who have let us down, God will never break His promises. In fact, Scripture tells us that even if we are faithless, God will remain faithful because He cannot deny Himself (2 Tim. 2:11–13).

Take a moment to consider: In what ways have your disappointments affected your view of God? How does today's text challenge your view of God?

The best way to understand the loving and trustworthy heart of God is to look at the life of Jesus, who makes the Father known. When we were still His enemies, Jesus Christ left the glories of heaven to come dwell among us, live with us, and die for us (Rom. 5:8 and 1 John 4:10).

As we spend time getting to know Jesus, we get to know the loving heart of God. We may not always understand God. (After all, how could any of us grasp the enormity of His heavenly plans?) And sometimes, we might expect Him to act one way and be disappointed when He acts differently. But in the words of an old hymn, God is "too wise to be mistaken" and "too good to be unkind."[11] When we cannot trace His hand, we must trust His heart.[12]

God keeps His promises. Always. You can count on it.

Feast at the table

If you have more time to linger at the breakfast table, open your Bible and let's FEAST on God's Word together!

Focus on God

Open your Bible and read Isaiah 55:11. What do you want to say to God as you begin today's study?

Engage the Text

Turn to Numbers 23:13–26 and read it out loud.

Balak was the king of Moab, a country bent on destroying Israel, God's chosen people. He believed there was no military way to defeat Israel, so he sent for Balaam, a diviner with an international reputation who used sorcery and pagan methods to conjure the gods. Balak charged Balaam to curse the Israelites. In Numbers 23:1–12, Balaam has his first encounter with God, which doesn't go as Balak had hoped. Based on 23:11, what happened the first time Balaam tried to curse the Israelites?

Today's passage describes his second attempt. King Balak has a specific agenda in mind and charges Balaam to carry it out. What outcome is Balak hoping for (see verse 13)?

What had God promised Abraham in Genesis 12:2–3, hundreds of years before the encounter described in today's text?

What does Balaam's response to Balak in Numbers 23:19–20 reveal about God's character?

This is the second of Balaam's three attempts to curse the Israelites at Balak's request. Skip forward to Numbers 24:9–10. How does Balaam fulfill God's promise to Abraham?

Back to our text, in Numbers 23:21, who does Balaam describe as Israel's king? What are a king's responsibilities?

What does Balaam end up saying about the Israelites in verses 21–24? Would this be considered a curse or a blessing?

How do Balaam's words affect King Balak (see verse 25)?

As you consider this entire passage, what does this text demonstrate about God's commitment to His people? About His faithfulness?

Assess the Main Idea

In a single sentence, summarize what this text teaches about God.

Spark Transformation

What circumstances in your life cause you to question God's love and faithfulness? What's the worst-case scenario you can picture in your life?

Read 2 Timothy 2:11–13. What does this passage say about God?

On a piece of paper, write out "Even if _____ [fill in the blank with your worst-case situation], God will STILL be faithful to His promises." Post that sentence somewhere you will see it and be reminded to trust in God.

Turn to God in Worship

This story with Balak and Balaam happened during Israel's wandering in the desert for forty years because of disobeying God. Yet despite their disobedience, God remained faithful to His promise to bless them. Spend a few minutes worshiping God for His steadfastness, His faithfulness, His trustworthiness, and His unchanging love. Meditate on His character, and then praise Him for the ways those characteristics have been evident in your own life.

 *Freezer-friendly*

One pie crust (you can buy these
   frozen at the store, or make your
   own from scratch)

6 large eggs, room temperature

12 pieces of turkey bacon, cooked
   and diced

1 cup Swiss cheese, grated

1 cup kale, torn into bite-sized pieces

3 green onions, chopped

1 cup heavy cream

1 cup half and half

1/4 tsp sugar (can omit for
   sugar-free recipe)

1/8 tsp ground cayenne pepper

1/8 tsp sea salt

1/8 tsp ground turmeric

1. Preheat oven to 425° F.

2. Lay crust in a deep-dish pie dish and then spread bacon, cheese, kale, and green onions, stirring gently to combine.

2. In a medium bowl, whisk together remaining ingredients and pour over top of quiche filling.

3. Bake for 15 minutes, then lower temperature to 300° F and bake until a knife inserted into the center comes out clean, about 30 minutes.

4. And pray over it 'cuz I thought it turned out yummy, and I know that's why: God blessed it. (Seriously, that's part of the recipe!)

Optional: Double this recipe and freeze the extra portion for another day. First allow the baked quiche to cool completely, and then wrap in plastic wrap and aluminum foil. When ready to serve, thaw quiche in the fridge , remove plastic wrap and foil, and reheat at 300° F until heated through, about 15 minutes.

Power Prayer Quiche Lorraine

Okay, I know the name of this recipe sounds kind of hokey, but it's how I'll forever think of it. You see, I've tried so many disappointing quiches that I'd given up hope of ever finding one I like. And then one day I attended a prayer gathering with some of my very dearest friends and prayer warriors. And you guys—the smell of these quiches filled the house in the most amazing way. After a time of prayer, we all partook of the fabulous brunch my friend had coordinated for us, and I cautiously took a bite of this quiche—and I heard angels singing. Or something close to that, because I went back for another slice, and took another slice home, and then texted my friend to ask for the recipe because it was that good.

DAY 7
The Whole Thing

 Snack on the go

I'm fascinated by the story of the rich young ruler in the Bible. Here comes a man running to Jesus, falling to His feet, and asking how he might inherit eternal life. He's kept the Ten Commandments since he was a young boy, and he's eager to follow the rules. For any of us mamas, this sounds like a suitable candidate for a son-in-law, am I right?

Jesus looked at him, loved him, and told him to sell his possessions, give the proceeds to the poor, and follow Him (Mark 10:17–27). Strikingly, it's Jesus' *love* that compels Him to instruct him so; He didn't speak out of spite. There were other rich people following Jesus, but He only instructs this one to part with his riches, because He loved him. Yet the young man walked away saddened, because he was unwilling to part with his riches.

In this vignette, as throughout Scripture, we see that God's love compels ALL of our devotion: "Love the Lord your God with all your heart and with all your soul and with all your strength" (Deut. 6:5).

When we hold back from God, we rob only ourselves. He continues loving us, but we miss out on experiencing the richness of His grace, the joy of His presence, the sufficiency of His mercy.

God wants us to love Him with all we've got. On our own, this kind of love would be impossible, but Jesus teaches us how to love by first loving us. The Good Shepherd leaves the ninety-nine to go after the one lost lamb. The Living Water quenches the thirst of the parched who come to Him. The Lion of Judah goes to war to defeat the enemy of our souls.

He offers us everything He is, but anything that comes between us and the Lover of our souls must go. Picture Jesus looking at you with His loving gaze. Is there anything He's asking you to let go of today?

Hold nothing back, friend. It may seem costly at first, but when we give Him all we are, we receive in exchange all He is and has for us.

 Feast at the table | *If you have more time to linger at the breakfast table, open your Bible and let's FEAST on God's Word together!*

Focus on God

Open your Bible to Psalm 139:23–24 and pray through these verses to focus your heart and mind on God as you begin.

Engage the Text

Read Deuteronomy 6:4–9 out loud. Read it again, emphasizing the key words in today's text.

Read it one more time, louder this time, with greater inflection in your voice, with conviction and power.

What changed for you as you read the passage each time?

Today's text is known as the *Shema*, based on the Hebrew word for "hear," and it's recited as part of Jewish morning and evening prayers. Why do you think they would choose this passage for their daily recitations?

What does verse 4 say about God?

How is this different from the polytheistic (i.e., many gods) culture that would have surrounded the Israelites in Canaan?

Today's passage comes right after the giving of the Ten Commandments in chapter 5. According to verses 6–9, what were the people to do with the commandments?

What are the Israelites commanded to do in verse 5?

How does love affect obedience?

What would obedience without love look like?

What is the significance of this threefold love (heart, soul, strength)?

Turn your Bible to Mark 12:29–31. What does Jesus say about all the other commandments in this passage?

How does Jesus' quotation of Deuteronomy affirm our greatest responsibility of love toward God and others?

According to Paul in 1 Corinthians 13, how does our love for God affect our love for others?

Assess the Main Idea

Summarize the main idea of Deuteronomy 6:4–9 in a single sentence.

Spark Transformation

In the space below, explain how you can love God with all your heart, with all your soul, and with all your strength.

Take a moment to ponder: Are you holding any area of your life back from God? Ask the Holy Spirit to help you surrender everything to Him in adoration, that you may love Him and others as He desires.

Turn to God in Worship

We learn what love looks like when we gaze into the beauty of Love Himself, because God is love (1 John 4:8), and Jesus demonstrated love in laying His life down for us. Read 1 Corinthians 13 again, this time replacing the word "love" with the name "Jesus" (e.g., "Jesus is patient." "Jesus is kind.")

Take your time with this, and allow the words to direct your heart toward Him in worship. Pause after you say each phrase, and call to mind situations in Scripture and in your own life when you've experienced the love of God. End your time in worship by thanking the Father for giving us His Son in love so that we would learn how to better love Him and love each other.[13]

What stood out to you in today's devotional? Share with us on social media with the hashtag #bibleandbreakfast.

Develop a Healthy Habit

Take a few moments to reflect on the past week and celebrate your progress. You may be surprised by what you learn, and you'll be more likely to be consistent in your new habit.

What have you learned about Jesus so far?

What are you enjoying about your *Bible and Breakfast* habit?

What's not working so well with your *Bible and Breakfast* habit, or what would you like to do differently?

What tweaks can you make to your morning time with Jesus to create a stronger and more enjoyable habit?

What would you like to say to Jesus as you reflect on the past week together? In the space below, write a few words of worship, praise, gratitude, or rededication.

❄ *Freezer-friendly*

⊘ *Gluten-free*

✋ *Kid-friendly*

_____

2 large eggs

$1/2$ cup maple syrup

$1/4$ cup coconut oil, melted

$1/2$ cup applesauce

1 $1/2$ cups milk

2 tsp vanilla

3 cups rolled oats

2 tsp baking powder

$1/2$ tsp salt

1 $1/2$ tsp cinnamon

Toppings of choice: berries, banana slices, nuts, dried fruit, chocolate chips

1. Preheat oven to 350° F and line muffin tin with foil liners or spray with cooking spray. This batter will get sticky while baked.

2. Whisk wet ingredients in a large bowl. Stir in oats, baking powder, salt, and cinnamon until well blended.

3. Using an ice cream scoop or a large spoon, fill each muffin tin with $1/4$ cup oat mixture.

4. Top with your favorite toppings, pushing slightly into oat mixture with the back of a spoon.

5. Bake until firm, about 30 minutes. Allow to cool for 5 minutes before removing to a wire rack to cool completely.

To-Go Baked Oatmeal Cups

I love how versatile these little oatmeal cups can be! The kids especially have fun mixing different toppings to make their own unique creations. Use whatever fruit is in season, or combine toppings to imitate your favorite dessert. Try chopped apples and nutmeg for an apple pie oatmeal cup; bananas and browned butter for banana foster; almonds, coconut, and chocolate chips for a popular candy bar; or strawberries and cream cheese for a cheesecake variation. Your only limit is your imagination!

DAY 8
Savor

 Snack on the go

If you're in a rush, the short devotional below is a quick "spiritual snack" to feed your soul and meditate on all day long.

Have you ever felt desperate? In my own life, sometimes it's been my eating habits. Other times it's been relationships. Or finances. Or a health crisis.

Whatever the cause, our desperation can open us to God's deliverance. In Mark 7:32–35 we read of a man who experienced God's life-changing work in unconventional ways:

> There some people brought to him a man who was deaf and could hardly talk, and they begged Jesus to place his hand on him.
>
> After he took him aside, away from the crowd, Jesus put his fingers into the man's ears. Then he spit and touched the man's tongue. He looked up to heaven and with a deep sigh said to him, "Ephphatha!" (which means "Be opened!"). At this, the man's ears were opened, his tongue was loosened and he began to speak plainly.

This encounter is incredibly personal. Though Jesus could have healed this man with a word and then moved right along, He gave this desperate man His individual attention.

But it's also a bit weird. Spit? Sighing? Most people may have been put off by Jesus' methods, but not this man; though he may not have understood Jesus' methods, he trusted Jesus and was healed immediately.

As you reflect on your own life, have you ever questioned God's methods of dealing with you? Has personal desperation made you more open to God's work? Is it possible that the weird things in your life right now might actually indicate His loving hand at work?

Sit for a minute with Jesus this morning. Before you rush on to what your day holds, slow down, and picture Him pulling you away from the crowd, away from the day's demands. Imagine His healing hand touching the broken parts of your body and life.

Now hear Jesus praying for you. His voice is low, a deep sigh spoken quietly but powerfully over your life. Read Jesus' prayer in John 17:13–26, and let His words wash over you, bringing healing to any broken places.

 Feast at the table | *If you have more time to linger at the breakfast table, open your Bible and let's FEAST on God's Word together!*

Focus on God

Open your Bible and read Psalm 119:130. Ask the Holy Spirit to sanctify your imagination and open the eyes of your heart to understand and receive His Word.

Engage the Text

Read Mark 7:31–37 out loud, marking any words that stick out to you.

Read it again, more slowly this time, pausing after each verse to picture the scene in your mind. Imagine you're watching this story as a movie, and identify the sounds, the smells, the sensations of each action as it takes place.

What stands out to you?

Read the passage again, focusing on Jesus' actions. How does He react to the crowds?

What does He do first?

How does He interact with the man brought to Him?

What do His actions say about His character?

Now read the text one more time, seeing the crowd move as one fluid mass from beginning to end, with a group of people pushing up front to bring their friend to Jesus. What were they hoping for?

What did they witness?

What was their reaction to the miracle?

Read the passage once more (yeah, I know this is a lot of rereading, but it's a short passage), and put yourself in the deaf man's place. Use your sanctified imagination to picture this. What thoughts would be going through his mind as his friends brought him to Jesus?

What fears and hopes?

What emotions as healing takes place?

What words would he have spoken first?

What would he have done for the rest of the day?

Finally, read the passage, one last time, allowing God's Spirit to bring the words to life as you linger on anything else you notice in the text.

Assess the Main Idea

What theme or image jumped out to you as you read and reread this passage?

What characteristic of Jesus stood out as you interacted with this text?

Spark Transformation

Mull over this scene, savoring it for a few minutes, talking to God about it.

Allow the beauty of Jesus as revealed in this passage to work on your heart. Close your eyes and picture Him in your mind's eye. We become like the ones we spend time with, so simply rest in Jesus' presence and meditate on His character. Move into a time of quiet, rest, and yielding to God, asking Him to transform you into the image of His Son.

Turn to God in Worship

End your time by worshiping Jesus of Nazareth, God-become-man, revealed in the pages of Scripture. He is as alive today as He was 2,000 years ago. Spend time with Him. Bask in His presence as you wrap up this time together and allow His quiet and rest to follow you throughout your day.

Today's FEAST was a little different, wasn't it? Did it make you feel a little uncomfortable? Or was it a welcome break from our typical study prompts? In my own life, I've found that I often get in a rut in my Bible study, engaging Scripture with the left side of my brain as I read it analytically, approaching the Word as only a text to be studied instead of a person to get to know.

⊘ *Gluten-free*
☑ *Meal Prep*

---

2 cups quinoa, rinsed

4 cups chicken stock

1 Tbsp olive oil

1 large onion, chopped

4 uncooked sausage links, sliced

4 large eggs

2 avocados, sliced

1 cup grape tomatoes, halved

Salt and pepper to taste

Drizzle of balsamic glaze, optional

Sprinkling of cheese of choice,
   optional

1. Stir quinoa and chicken stock into a small pot; cover and bring to a boil. Turn heat to low and simmer for 15 minutes. Fluff with a fork and let cool for 5 minutes.

2. In the meantime, sauté onion in olive oil over medium-low heat until softened, then stir in the sausage slices and cook until no longer pink. (To meal prep, cook through step 2 and layer quinoa and onion-sausage mixture in a freezer-safe container. When ready to serve, remove the cover and microwave to defrost the quinoa base, about a minute. Top with remaining ingredients.)

3. Divide quinoa equally among four bowls and top with onion-sausage mixture to one side. Arrange avocado slices and tomato halves in the bowls.

4. Cook eggs however you'd like (fried, scrambled, poached, or boiled) and add to quinoa bowls.

5. Top with a drizzle of balsamic glaze and a sprinkling of your favorite cheese, if using. I prefer sharp Cheddar, but goat cheese is a lovely alternative.

Quinoa Breakfast Bowls

When my husband was going through a serious quinoa-loving phase, this recipe did not disappoint. It's more of a guide than an actual recipe, but it's easy to adapt to whatever you'd like.

DAY 9
Wholesome

 Snack on the go | *If you're in a rush, the short devotional below is a quick "spiritual snack" to feed your soul and meditate on all day long.*

Did your mom ever say to you, "If you can't say something nice, don't say anything at all"?

I find myself saying these very words to my own children, whether I'm breaking up squabbles, putting the brakes on bragging, or simply calling out meanness. It's amazing how early children develop the ability to lash out in anger, saying hurtful things to one another—and to us.

As easy as it is to correct children, it's much harder to identify and correct our own harmful words. We justify ourselves, explaining that we yelled at our kids because they wouldn't listen, we swore at the driver because he almost hit us, or we gossiped about that coworker because, "well, I was just telling the truth."

But Scripture holds us to a much higher standard: "Do not let any unwholesome talk come out of your mouths, but only what is helpful for building others up according to their needs, that it may benefit those who listen" (Eph. 4:29).

Only what is helpful, the Bible says.

As a young woman, I once heard someone share this internal filter for what to say and what to leave unsaid:

1. Is it true?

2. Is it kind?

3. Is it necessary?

These questions help us pause and consider the effects of our words instead of spewing whatever comes to mind. But when we consider this next verse in context, we see that our speech is to reflect the character of Jesus: "Be kind and compassionate to one another, forgiving each other, just as in Christ God forgave you" (Eph. 4:32).

Why should we speak kindly? Why show compassion in our speech and actions? Because of Jesus.

Jesus changes everything. When we spend time with Him—getting to know Him through the Gospel narratives, talking with Him throughout our day, listening to His Spirit within us—we begin to be like Him because we've been with Him.

Who do you struggle to speak kindly to? Write a short prayer below, asking the Lord Jesus to help you speak as He would speak to this person, building them up with true, kind, and necessary encouragement.

 Feast at the table | *If you have more time to linger at the breakfast table, open your Bible and let's FEAST on God's Word together!*

Focus on God

Open your Bible to James 1:22 and ask God to help you be open to living out His Word today.

Engage the Text

Read Ephesians 4:29–32 out loud. Write down any observations that immediately come to mind.

Look up the passage in two or three other translations, and note any additional insights. (Using an online resource like biblegateway.com is a great way to read verses in several translations.)

Rewrite verse 29 below, using simple terms as if you were explaining it to a child.

What connection might there be between the sins listed in verse 31 and the unwholesome talk mentioned in verse 29?

How do these behaviors affect God (see verse 30)?

Paul appeals to Jesus as the model for how Christians are to love and speak to one another (see Eph. 4:32 and Eph. 5:1–2). How does Jesus speak to His disciples throughout Scripture? (Hint: John 13–17 is a gold mine.) List several examples that come to mind.

How does Jesus speak to His enemies (see Luke 22:47–53)?

According to this text, what do spoken words reveal about what's in one's heart?

Assess the Main Idea

Write the main point of this passage in a sentence.

Spark Transformation

How have others spoken "unwholesomely" toward you in the past? Do you need to forgive them, as God forgave you?

Ask God's Spirit to reveal to you specific situations over the last 48 hours in which your words have torn down another person. Is there someone you need to ask forgiveness from? Ask God to put a guard over your mouth (Ps. 141:3) and to help you speak words of kindness and compassion.

Turn to God in Worship

Spend a few moments thanking God for His forgiveness in Jesus Christ, and for His kindness that compels us to be kind toward others. Dedicate your words to God, to be used by Him to build others up.

| PREP TIME: *10 minutes* | COOK TIME: *none* | YIELD: *8 servings* |

⊘ *Gluten-free*

✋ *Kid-friendly*

☑ *Meal Prep*

---

8 large eggs, hard-boiled and peeled

2 Tbsp mayonnaise

2 Tbsp cream cheese, softened

2 Tbsp EACH green onions, celery, red bell pepper, or veggies of choice, diced

Salt and pepper to taste

1. Using a box grater, grate the eggs into a bowl.

2. Stir in the rest of your ingredients until well-blended. The egg yolks will blend in with the mayo and cream cheese making the smash creamy and delicious.

3. Serve on your favorite toasted bread.

Egg and Veggie Smash on Toast

I've heard variations of this recipe called "egg salad," but the word salad makes me think of romaine lettuce and vegetables, which this is decidedly not. But this recipe is endlessly versatile, and you can stir in your favorite veggies for a colorful and healthy breakfast spread. And let's face it, smashing something for breakfast just sounds fun, doesn't it? For a healthier alternative, substitute mashed (or smashed!) avocado for the mayo and/or cream cheese. If you do, serve immediately as the avocado will eventually turn the smash brown.

DAY 10
Being Bold

 Snack on the go

Sometimes heroes in the Bible take on bigger-than-life proportions. Imagine the faith of David as he walked up to the giant, or the courage of Rahab as she hid the spies, or the bravery of the sinful woman as she anointed Jesus.

But Scripture portrays a much more nuanced portrait of these biblical heroes, describing their fears and failures along with their faith. In fact, the Bible tells us that God chooses people not because they are great but because their weaknesses are the perfect canvas for Him to display His power (1 Cor. 1:27).

One such example is found in Timothy, Paul's young protégé. Although he had grown up with a mom and grandma who taught him about Jesus, and although Paul had been training him to become a church leader, Timothy lacked confidence. In one of his personal letters, Paul writes to him: "For God gave us a spirit not of fear but of power and love and self-control. Therefore do not be ashamed of the testimony about our Lord" (2 Tim. 1:7–8a ESV).

Isn't it reassuring to know that even Timothy struggled with fear and timidity? Yet God used him to continue the work of the gospel among the churches Paul had planted, because Timothy believed and lived through God's Spirit of power, love, and self-discipline within him.

In fact, elsewhere in Scripture we're told that "the Spirit of him who raised Jesus from the dead is living in you" (Rom. 8:11) and that the same Spirit works in us love and self-control, among other things (Gal. 5:22–23).

As you look at your own life, what fears hold you back from boldly talking about Jesus? How might God use the weaknesses in your life to show His power?

Jesus invites you to join Him in welcoming others into the family of God. He wants to use you. Yes, you. What emotions does this invitation awaken in you?

Grab a pen and write "power, love, and self-control" on a sticky note or on your hand to remind yourself today of the ways Jesus is working through His Spirit in your life to draw others to Himself.

 **Feast at the table** *If you have more time to linger at the breakfast table, open your Bible and let's FEAST on God's Word together!*

Focus on God

Open your Bible to Psalm 119:160. As you read, use the words to guide you in an opening prayer, asking God to give you spiritual understanding as you study His Word.

Engage the Text

Read 2 Timothy 1:6–10 out loud.

Write down a verse that stands out to you.

What does Paul instruct Timothy to do with his gift?

Who is the gift from?

How did Timothy receive it?

Now look at verse 7 again. What two types of spirits does Paul contrast?

Look up the cross-references for "timidity" (if needed, you can find the cross-references online at biblegateway.com or biblehub.com). List a few passages below, and write down how each illuminates an aspect of the timidity Timothy was facing.

Based on these readings, what would have caused Timothy's timidity?

In contrast, what kind of truth does Paul exhort Timothy to acknowledge in his life (see verses 8–10)?

Notice that Paul affirms to Timothy what is already true of him, and encourages him to live in light of that truth. This isn't merely positive self-talk or some psycho mumbo-jumbo Paul's talking about. According to verses 8–9, how does Paul describe God's work in Timothy's life?

How do these foundational realities affect the spirit of power, love, and self-discipline that ought to characterize Timothy's actions?

Assess the Main Idea

Write down the main idea of the passage in a single sentence.

Spark Transformation

What fears are you facing in your life? What threatens to make you timid, holding back from speaking boldly and lovingly about the grace of Jesus Christ?

Are there any past mistakes or false accusations or misunderstandings that make you hesitate to "fan into flame" the gift that God has given you?

Take some time today to talk about these things with God, and ask Him to help you live in the fullness of His Spirit today.

Turn to God in Worship

Look again at verses 9–10. Use these Scriptures to voice your thanksgiving to God:

> Father, I praise You for saving me and calling me to a holy life, not because of my good track record, but because of Your own purpose and grace. Thank You for revealing Your grace through Jesus Christ and for Your victory in defeating death and bringing life and immortality to light through the gospel. I praise You for rescuing me from my greatest fears, and thank You that because of Jesus, I have nothing to fear. Thank You for filling me with Your Spirit and for working in me Your power, love, and self-control. Amen.

What stood out to you in today's devotional? Share with us on social media: #bibleandbreakfast.

| **PREP TIME:** *10 minutes* | **COOL TIME:** *30 minutes* | **YIELD:** *20 power balls* |

❄️ *Freezer-friendly*

⊘ *Gluten-free*

✋ *Kid-friendly*

☑️ *Meal Prep*

---

1 cup rolled oats

1/2 cup almond meal

1/4 cup flaxseed

2 tsp chia seeds

2/3 cup unsweetened coconut
  flakes, toasted

1/2 tsp cinnamon

1/2 cup mini chocolate chips
  (sugar-free optional)

1/3 cup raw peanut butter

1/2 cup raw almond butter

1/4 cup raw honey

1 tsp vanilla extract

1. In a large bowl, stir together dry ingredients. Make a well in the center, and add the liquid ingredients. Stir until well incorporated.

2. Refrigerate mixture until firm enough to handle, about 20 minutes. Meanwhile, clean up the kitchen, and sit down with Jesus and today's Snack or FEAST of the day.

3. Use a spoon to scoop out the mixture and roll into 1-inch balls.

4. Store in an airtight container for up to 2 weeks (if they last that long). You can also freeze these for up to 3 months. Just allow to thaw for a few minutes before you take a bite.

Sugarfast Power Balls

Whether you call them power balls, energy bites, protein bites, or something else, these little balls of deliciousness have taken over the internet. But most recipes I've found include protein powder, which has a decidedly chalky taste, so I resisted making them for years. But in the middle of my second 40-day sugar fast,[14] my dear friend Wendy surprised me by mailing half a dozen of these sweet treats across the country and they showed up at my door at just the right time—and I was surprised how much I liked them! This version includes a medley of some of our favorite things.

DAY 11
Enjoy

 **Snack on the go** | *If you're in a rush, the short devotional below is a quick "spiritual snack" to feed your soul and meditate on all day long.*

What's your purpose in life?

Now there's a philosophical question to get your morning started! But take a moment to step back and reflect on that question, then write a brief answer below:

Throughout history, thousands of people have memorized the answer to that opening question as it's written in the Westminster Shorter Catechism: "Man's chief end is to glorify God and to enjoy Him for ever."[15]

The Bible is replete with instruction to glorify God; in fact, your answer above may have even included some variation of the word "glorify" if you spent much time in Sunday school as a child.

It's the second part of that answer that's surprising, though, even for those of us who've grown up in the church. Enjoy God? What does that look like?

In Psalm 16:11 (ESV), we find David saying this of God: "You make known to me the path of life; in your presence there is fullness of joy; at your right hand are pleasures forevermore."

Did you catch that? Our path of life, our joy, and our eternal pleasures are all found in the presence of God Himself. Not in retail therapy, not in status likes, not in a promotion, not in weight loss. But in Christ alone.

As one pastor puts it: "God is most glorified in us when we are most satisfied in Him."[16] God's glory is intimately connected to our joy, which we find only in Jesus Christ: "These things I have spoken to you, that my joy may be in you, and that your joy may be full" (John 15:11 esv).

Everything we need we already have in Jesus. And because our joy is in Him, we can enjoy God and glorify Him forever.

Even today? Yes, even today.

As you finish your breakfast, picture Jesus sitting next to you. Relish His presence. In what ways is He inviting you to find your joy in Him alone?

 Feast at the table | *If you have more time to linger at the breakfast table, open your Bible and let's FEAST on God's Word together!*

Focus on God

Open your Bible to 2 Timothy 3:16–17 and write it in the space below, personalizing it with your name after each descriptor of God's Word. (For example, "useful for teaching [insert your name], rebuking [insert your name] . . .")

Engage the Text

Read Psalm 16 out loud. What observations immediately jump out to you?

In your notebook, make two columns: in the first, note all the things David does or promises to do; in the second, note everything God does.

Compare David's and God's actions. How are they similar? How are they different?

What does David pray for in verse 1?

How does God answer David's prayer, according to verse 11?

Beyond mere safety and survival, what else does God provide for David?

Assess the Main Idea

The unifying theme of this psalm is the joy righteous people enjoy in God's presence. What does this say about God?

Summarize the main idea in a single sentence.

Spark Transformation

What situation do you need to trust God with today?

Surrender this situation to Him, declaring His trustworthiness in your life. Then, whenever you're tempted to worry about it throughout the day, pause and renew your commitment to trust God. You might even read the psalm again out loud, making it your declaration of trust in God.

Turn to God in Worship

The ancient Greeks and Romans offered sacrifices to secure their false gods' good graces, hoping these temperamental gods would act in their favor. In contrast, the true God whom we serve is steadfast, and His love is unchanging.

Read through the psalm once more, noting the characteristics of God revealed in the text, and then praise Him for who He is. (For example, verse 1: "Thank You for keeping me safe, O God; thank You for welcoming me to seek refuge in You.")

 *Freezer-friendly*

 Kid-friendly

8 slices bacon, diced

1/3 cup finely chopped sweet onion

2 Tbsp green onions, chopped
  (plus more for topping)

2 cups corn

1 cup all-purpose flour

1 cup yellow cornmeal

2 tsp baking powder

1/4 tsp baking soda

1/2 tsp salt

1/4 tsp freshly ground pepper

1 1/4 cups milk

2 large eggs, beaten

2 Tbsp oil, plus more for oiling griddle

1 cup freshly grated sharp Cheddar
  cheese

Warm maple syrup, for serving

1. Cook the bacon in skillet over medium-high heat until it begins to brown, then add the onions and corn and continue to cook until bacon is crisp and onion is soft. Take a moment to close your eyes and whiff the glorious smell as it fills your house and try to avoid burning your tongue as you taste this delicious mixture. Set aside a spoonful of bacon mixture for topping.

2. Meanwhile, combine dry ingredients in a medium bowl. Make a well in the middle and stir together the wet ingredients. Add the corn mixture and gently fold it all together. Don't over mix—we're going for rustic "griddle" cakes here.

3. Preheat griddle over medium-low heat for 5 minutes. You'll know it's hot enough when you sprinkle some water on it and hear it sizzle. Grease griddle and spoon 1/4 cup batter, spreading it into an even circle. Cook until golden brown on both sides, about 3 to 4 minutes per side.

4. Stack cooked pancakes on a wire rack and keep in a warm oven while you finish cooking the remaining pancakes.

5. Serve with a sprinkling of reserved bacon mixture and extra green onions for a dash of color. Top with warm maple syrup and a sunny-side up fried egg for a complete breakfast.

Savory Bacon and Corn Pancakes

Bacon, corn, cheese, and maple syrup—basically a match made in heaven for my husband, who prefers savory over sweet for breakfast. The first time I made these was for a church beach brunch. I remember the wind whipping my hair as I munched happily on these pancakes. Unfortunately, I had undercooked them and the middle was still a bit doughy, but they were still so good they disappeared in minutes. So, cook these all the way through, and eat them in the sunshine!

DAY 12
Coming Home

 Snack on the go

Have you ever felt far from God, wondering, "Lord, where are You?"

The Israelites did. As Babylonian prisoners of war, they voiced their despair in this psalm:

> *By the rivers of Babylon we sat and wept*
> *when we remembered Zion.*
> *There on the poplars*
> *we hung our harps,*
> *for there our captors asked us for songs,*
> *our tormentors demanded songs of joy;*
> *they said, "Sing us one of the songs of Zion!"*
>
> *How can we sing the songs of the LORD*
> *while in a foreign land? (Ps. 137:1–4)*

The Israelites were in exile because they had rejected God. Their homes were ruined, their families killed, their freedoms stolen, and their hopes dashed. Did God still care?

Even though their circumstances were dire, God did not forget His people. Through His prophet Jeremiah, God spoke to the exiles in Babylon:

> *This is what the LORD says: "When seventy years are completed for Babylon, I will come to you and fulfill my good promise to bring you back to this place. . . . Then you will call on me and come and pray to me, and I will listen to you. You will seek me and find me when you seek me with all your heart. I will be found by you," declares the LORD (Jer. 29:10, 12–14a).*

What a generous promise! God assured them that when they turned to seek Him with all their hearts, they would find Him. Because God is never far from those who seek Him (Acts 17:27).

This Old Testament story reveals how the Lord longs to be in close relationship with His children. He sent His own Son, Jesus, God-made-flesh, to walk among us and to welcome us into the family of God. And He has placed His own Spirit within us, that we may call out "Abba, Father" in our moments of need (Gal. 4:6–7).

Whatever you're feeling today, know that God is not far off. Even if you don't feel close to God, continue seeking Him. Keep reading the Bible because we all need Scripture to remind us what is true when our hearts lose their way.

If you're sad, seek God in your sadness.

If you're grieving, seek God in your grief.

If you're rejoicing, seek God in your joy.

Recognize your emotions and bring them to the Lord in prayer. He sees you. He hears you. And He cares for you.

Feast at the table

If you have more time to linger at the breakfast table, open your Bible and let's FEAST on God's Word together!

Focus on God

Open your Bible to Colossians 3:16, and turn it into a prayer in the space below.

Engage the Text

Read Jeremiah 29:10–14 out loud. This passage is often taken out of context and twisted to mean things it doesn't, so let's start by asking the five Ws. If you have a study Bible, you'll find notes at the beginning of the book of Jeremiah and possibly in the footnotes. You can also find study notes for this text in an online commentary like biblegateway.com or blueletterbible.com.

Who wrote this passage? When was it written?

What type of writing (genre) is it?

Where was it delivered (i.e., who was it written to?)?

Why was it written?

What does God promise to do in verses 10–11?

According to verses 12–13, what will the Israelites do?

How will God respond to the Israelites (see verses 12–14)?

Step back and skim the entire context of Jeremiah 29. What would verse 11 have meant for the original audience?

What does this passage say of God's character?

Assess the Main Idea

Jeremiah 29:10–14 is a promise written to a specific people in a specific situation. So having done the work of engaging the text through observations and reading some of the background of the passage, we move on to interpretation.

Can we take Jeremiah 29 and apply it directly to our lives today? Why or why not?

If you have read a commentary on this text for more insight into God's promises toward the Israelites and modern applications for Christians today, what did you learn?

Summarize the main idea of the passage in a single sentence.

Spark Transformation

How does this passage apply to your life today?

Have you learned something about God's character? About the way He treats rebellious children? About the way He thinks about and plans for His children? How do these truths change you?

Turn to God in Worship

Spend a few moments worshiping God for what you learned about Him today.

Wow, that was a lot of questions, wasn't it? I'd love to hear—how did it go for you? Is there anything you got stuck on? Did you have any aha moments? Share with us at #bibleandbreakfast.

⊘ *Gluten-free*

☑ *Meal Prep*

1 Tbsp butter

1 lb mushrooms, cleaned and sliced

2 garlic cloves, minced

2 Tbsp chopped green onion, plus
   extra for topping

Salt and pepper, to taste

8 large eggs

2 Tbsp heavy cream

¼ cup grated Swiss cheese,
   optional

1. Heat butter over medium-high heat in a large skillet. Add mushrooms and cook, stirring often, until they begin to sweat.

2. Stir in garlic and green onions and cook 5–8 minutes, until mushrooms are tender. Season with salt and pepper. Turn heat down to low. (To meal prep, prepare through step 2, cool, and store in an airtight container for up to 5 days. When ready to finish, reheat the mushroom mixture in a skillet on low and continue with step 3.)

3. Crack eggs in a medium bowl and beat with a fork until well-scrambled. Beat in heavy cream, salt, and pepper.

4. Pour eggs over mushrooms and cook over low heat. At first, it will look like nothing's happening, but keep a close eye on the eggs, and when the bottom of the pan is no longer translucent, stir the eggs in long strokes to allow ribbons to form.

5. Cook until no longer translucent, remove from heat, and serve with a sprinkling of green onions and cheese, if desired.

Sautéed Mushrooms and Eggs

When I was a child, our family home was seated on the fringe of a massive forest. The spring rains and peeking sun caused mushrooms to sprout under wet leaves, and many local villagers would forage the wild mushrooms and sell them that same day. This is the dish my mom would make on those sunny days following spring showers, and it's one I love to recreate, even if it's just with plain white mushrooms from my local grocer nowadays.

DAY 13
Just a "Peace"

 Snack on the go | *If you're in a rush, the short devotional below is a quick "spiritual snack" to feed your soul and meditate on all day long.*

From the moment our feet hit the floor, we're assaulted by headlines, checklists, and worries that steal our peace. It seems I can hardly make it to breakfast before I've found something or someone to worry about.

This morning, what worries are weighing heavy on your mind? List them in the space below:

It's easy to feel weighed down by our worries, but Jesus offers us something entirely different.

In Jesus' last conversation with His disciples, He says: "Peace I leave with you; my peace I give you" (John 14:27). Jesus offers us peace in the midst of the storms of life, inviting us to rest in Him just as He slept in the bottom of the boat in the middle of a storm (Mark 4:38–40).

But how do we embrace that peace? Practically speaking, when we scroll our newsfeeds and hear of the latest shooting, the impending storms, the financial collapse, how do we live at peace?

Isaiah 26:3 lays it out for us: "You will keep in perfect peace those whose minds are steadfast, because they trust in you."

Notice that perfect peace comes only from God; He is the One who offers the wholeness, quiet, and tranquility that settle our souls. But this peace is ours only when we lean into God, focusing our minds on Him.

Paul explains it this way: "Do not be anxious about anything, but in every situation, by prayer and petition, with thanksgiving, present your requests to God. And the peace of God, which transcends all understanding, will guard your hearts and your minds in Christ Jesus" (Phil. 4:6–7).

When we're tempted to fret, we can bring those situations before God, with our requests and our thanks. In exchange, God promises to guard our hearts and minds with His peace, a peace that surpasses human understanding.

As needed throughout the day, talk to God about each worry you listed. What can you thank Him for in each situation? What can you ask Him to do in those situations? As you present each situation, leave them at His feet and invite His peace to guard your heart and mind.

Feast at the table

If you have more time to linger at the breakfast table, open your Bible and let's FEAST on God's Word together!

Focus on God

Open your Bible to Hebrews 4:12 and rewrite it in the space below, thanking God for the power of His Word.

Engage the Text

Read Isaiah 26:1–9 out loud. Write down your observations about the text. What stands out to you?

This chapter is a song of praise in a book of prophecy. The phrase "in that day" refers to the Day of the Lord, which is often interpreted to mean the Messianic age when the Lord Jesus will literally rule the earth when He returns with judgment and victory. What parts of this text seem to point to a time in the future?

What verses seem to indicate timeless principles that are applicable in any era?

How does trusting God affect one's disposition (in verse 3)?

What does the writer charge others to do in verse 4? What reason does he give for this exhortation?

What characteristics of God are most evident in His actions, described in verses 4–7? How do these characteristics reinforce the assertions in verses 3–4?

How do the righteous respond to God's deliverance (see verses 8–9)?

In what way does verse 9 illustrate the actions of "those whose minds are steadfast" in verse 3?

What do you learn about God's character in this text?

Assess the Main Idea

Since this chapter is a song, it's written poetically to praise God for His deliverance. Summarize the main idea of this passage in a single sentence.

Spark Transformation

In what ways have you personally experienced the truths of this passage? Think back on a time you trusted God and He came through for you. What happened?

Now think of the situations facing you today: the appointments, the tasks, the conversations, etc. One by one, entrust them to the Lord, asking Him to give you His peace and to center your mind on Him.

Turn to God in Worship

Praise God for His trustworthiness and for His willingness to carry all of our worries and concerns. Thank Him for being strong enough to handle even the most difficult situations, and praise Him specifically for ways He has worked in your life so far this week.

Develop a Healthy Habit

Take a few moments to reflect on the past week and celebrate your progress. You may be surprised by what you learn, and you'll be more likely to be consistent in your new habit.

What have you learned about Jesus so far?

What are you enjoying about your *Bible and Breakfast* habit?

What's not working so well with your *Bible and Breakfast* habit, or what would you like to do differently?

What tweaks can you make to your morning time with Jesus to create a stronger and more enjoyable habit?

What would you like to say to Jesus as you reflect on the past week together? In the space below, write a few words of worship, praise, gratitude, or rededication.

❄ *Freezer-friendly*

✋ *Kid-friendly*

☑ *Meal Prep*

---

12 large eggs

½ tsp salt

¼ tsp pepper

2 Tbsp unsalted butter

12 oz breakfast sausage or ham

1 cup shredded cheese of your
   choice

½ cup diced onion

½ cup diced red bell pepper

2 Tbsp chopped chives

4 oz cream cheese, softened

12 whole wheat tortillas

1. In a large mixing bowl, whisk together the eggs and add salt and pepper.

2. If using breakfast sausage, cook in a pan over medium heat until no longer pink. Drain the fat and set aside. Melt 1 tablespoon butter in the same pan and sauté veggies with a sprinkling of salt, until soft. Remove from pan and set aside with the ham or sausage in a bowl.

3. Melt another tablespoon of butter in the same pan and pour in the eggs. Cook over low heat, and when the bottom of the eggs have started to set, gently scrape with a spatula until egg has fully cooked but is still shiny.

4. Stir in the Cheddar cheese, veggies, and cooked sausage. Add additional salt and pepper if you'd like.

5. Smear cream cheese on each tortilla. Top each with a slice of ham (if using) and ½ cup cooked egg mixture, and then roll them up like burritos. Individually wrap them in aluminum foil, and allow to cool. Store in fridge for a few days or in the freezer for up to 3 months.

Make-Ahead Breakfast Burritos

This recipe is a family affair—every member has a job to do, and we put on some fun music while we cook. These breakfast burritos are my idea of grab-and-go breakfast for a day of writing, because they're packed with protein and keep me full and focused for the better part of the day. My husband also packs these in his lunch bag for breakfast on his way to work, and my daughters split a burrito between the two of them.

DAY 14
To-Do List

 Snack on the go

When you think of church rules, what dos and don'ts come to mind?

DO go to church each week.

DON'T steal.

DO read your Bible every day.

DON'T swear.

The list could go on and on, right? Even in Old Testament times, people lived under the heavy burden of hundreds of rules, meant to highlight human sinfulness and point to God's holiness. But the New Testament tells us that Jesus fulfilled all the Old Testament laws—yet still died the death of a sinner, so that through Him we may have the righteousness of God.

Because of Jesus, we are now free from the tyranny of the law: "So the law was our guardian until Christ came that we might be justified by faith. Now that this faith has come, we are no longer under a guardian" (Gal. 3:24–25). But even more than that, we are also free to reflect His glory, free to become more like Him.

Now the Lord is the Spirit, and where the Spirit of the Lord is, there is freedom. And we all, who with unveiled faces contemplate the Lord's glory, are being transformed into His image with ever-increasing glory, which comes from the Lord, who is the Spirit (2 Cor. 3:17–18).

Because of Jesus, we no longer need to live by a list of dos and don'ts. Instead, we're free to live as His Spirit leads us, becoming more and more like Jesus.

Imagine how your life would change if you exchanged your list of internal rules for freedom in Christ. Would you act differently? If yes, how so? If no, why not?

The good news of the gospel is that Jesus invites us into a relationship with Him led not by rules but by a love that grows deeper and fuller and changes us in ways that reveal more of Jesus to those around us.

Now, close your eyes and picture the glory of Jesus Christ surrounding you. Allow His presence to lift your spirit and free you from the tyranny of the rules you lug around like unwanted baggage. Let His freedom seep into the deepest parts of your soul, and breathe in the joy of His presence.

 *Feast at the table* | *If you have more time to linger at the breakfast table, open your Bible and let's FEAST on God's Word together!*

Focus on God

Open your Bible to Psalm 130:5 and ask God to give you a spirit of expectancy as you read today, helping you see Him in Scripture.

Engage the Text

Read 2 Corinthians 3:7–18 out loud. What observations and questions immediately come to mind?

To understand the historical background that Paul is referring to here, read Exodus 34:27–35. In your own words, summarize the story.

Why was Moses's face radiating?

How did the Israelites react? Why?

Why and when did Moses wear a veil?

Returning to our text today in 2 Corinthians, Paul states that both the ministry of law (the Ten Commandments) and the ministry of the Spirit came with God's glory. How did they both reflect this glory?

According to verse 9, how are these two ministries different?

How do verses 10–11 compare the law of the Old Testament and the freedom of the Spirit? Which is greater? Why is it greater?

Based on everything that he had already explained, what does Paul conclude in verse 12?

What extra explanation does Paul offer in verses 13–15, both for the veil that Moses wore in the Exodus account and the veil that his contemporaries experienced? How does this veil affect people's understanding of Jesus Christ?

What happens when someone turns to the Lord, according to verses 16–17?

Paul takes this account of Moses's radiant face and applies it to his contemporary believers in Jesus. What does verse 18 say about New Testament believers? What does it say about Jesus?

Assess the Main Idea

Summarize the main idea of the passage in a single sentence.

Spark Transformation

Moses's face would radiate whenever he spent time in God's presence, but this brilliance would fade. What does this word picture reveal about the effects on our hearts and lives (and maybe even faces) of spending time in God's presence?

Christians today enjoy a privilege that Israelites back in Moses's day did not: we have free access to God whenever we desire (Heb. 4:16), yet we often take this privilege for granted. Today, renew your commitment to seek God's face wholeheartedly and consistently.

Turn to God in Worship

Taking both the Exodus and 2 Corinthians passages together, what do they communicate about God's character? End your time FEASTing in Scripture by worshiping God for His brilliance revealed in Jesus Christ.

☑ *Meal Prep*

---

3 lbs baby spinach (this looks like a lot, but it wilts when boiled, so don't panic)

2 Tbsp butter

2 ½ Tbsp flour

2 garlic cloves, diced

2 cups milk, warmed

Salt and pepper to taste

4 large eggs, cooked as desired

Parmesan cheese, optional

1. Bring a large pot of water to boil, adding a dash of salt. Add half the spinach, using a wooden spoon to push the leaves down into the water until they wilt. Cook for a few minutes until soft, and then drain in a colander. Repeat with second half. When the spinach has cooled, press out the remaining water and roughly chop it with a knife or food processor.

2. To make the béchamel sauce, melt butter in a heavy-bottomed saucepan. Sprinkle in flour and garlic and stir, cooking until golden brown, about 2 minutes. Be careful not to burn the flour. Slowly pour in milk in a continuous stream, stirring continuously with a wooden spoon. Adding all the milk at once will result in blobs of unincorporated flour. Slow and steady is key.

3. Bring the mixture to a boil, and continue stirring while it thickens, about 5 minutes. You'll know the sauce is done when it coats the back of your wooden spoon. Add salt and pepper to taste. If using Parmesan cheese, sprinkle it in now and stir to melt.

4. Mix the chopped spinach into the béchamel sauce until well incorporated. Let rest while you move on to step 5.

5. Cook your eggs as you prefer. Spoon creamy spinach into bowls and top with eggs. Serve immediately.

Creamy Spinach and Eggs

One of my earliest memories of comfort food is Romanian creamed spinach with an egg nestled in the center. Now I know what you're thinking: spinach for breakfast? Before you write this off, I beg you to give it a try. The béchamel sauce brings an unbelievable creaminess to the dish, and the fried egg on top takes this from a dinner side dish to a delicious (and semi-healthy) breakfast. Give yourself plenty of time the first time you make this, because the béchamel sauce can be a bit tricky if you've never tried it before. But once you get the hang of it, you'll want to make this recipe again and again.

DAY 15
Seeking Him

 **Snack on the go** | *If you're in a rush, the short devotional below is a quick "spiritual snack" to feed your soul and meditate on all day long.*

Have you ever felt the Lord prompt you to drop what you're doing and kneel in prayer?

A still small voice pierces my flurry of activity with the whisper, "Seek My face." And often, the tyranny of the urgent makes me respond, "Just a moment. Let me finish this first." I'm too busy to stop at just that moment.

It's not until later, when I'm elbows-high in soap suds or trying to fit a too-small-shoe on a growing child's foot, that I'm reminded of the earlier prompting I had ignored: "Seek My face." But it feels too late.

Has that ever happened to you? We miss that special moment, and guilt rushes in, threatening to drive us farther from the Lord. Shame keeps us from turning to Him. And the enemy whispers lies that make us want to hide, like Adam and Eve in the garden long ago.

But unlike our ancestors, we don't have to stay hidden in fear, because "perfect love casts out fear" (1 John 4:18 ESV). In Jesus, we find forgiveness, mercy, and grace (Heb. 4:16). So in that very moment we're reminded of our earlier failure to answer His call, we can choose to turn and seek Him. Because the best time to seek the Lord is right now.

David attests to this truth in Psalm 27:8 (ESV): "You have said, 'Seek my face.' My heart says to you, 'Your face, LORD, do I seek.'"

This time seeking God's face may mean setting aside the phone for deeper Bible study, kneeling in your living room for a time of quiet prayer, or turning off the radio in the car to sing His praises instead.

Today, as we hear His Spirit call out to us, "Seek my face," let us be quick to respond. In fact, pause right now to breathe those words out loud: *Your face, LORD, do I seek.*

Write a prayer below asking God to make you more sensitive to His invitations to deeper fellowship and prompts to seek Him with all your heart.

 *Feast at the table*

If you have more time to linger at the breakfast table, open your Bible and let's FEAST on God's Word together!

Focus on God

Open your Bible to John 1:14, and write down a prayer asking God to help you see Jesus in today's passage.

Engage the Text

Read Psalm 27 out loud. Write out any observations that immediately come to mind.

What verse stands out to you the most? Write it below.

Why did you choose that verse?

What was David's one request of the Lord in verse 4?

What does this reveal about his deepest heart's desire?

God called David a man after His own heart (see Acts 13:22). What does this reveal about what God wants us to long for and desire the most?

Did David receive his one request? Which verses in this psalm speak to that answer?

Read Jeremiah 29:13, and compare it to verse 8 in today's psalm. What are the similarities?

Is this assurance limited to only the Israelites in the Old Testament or does it also extend to believers under the new covenant?

What does James 4:8 say about this question?

What else stood out to you in today's text?

Assess the Main Idea

Summarize the main theme of this psalm in a single sentence.

Spark Transformation

Can you honestly say that verse 4 is true of your life? If yes, ask God to continue to make it true and deepen your desire for Him. And if not, confess your apathy to God and ask Him to give you a burning desire for Him. Keep praying until you see the change you're asking for. Write a prayer in the space below.

Turn to God in Worship

What is true of God in this passage? Praise Him for the attributes you see in the psalm.

❄ *Freezer-friendly*

✋ *Kid-friendly*

☑ *Meal Prep*

_____

2 cups all-purpose flour

2 cups whole wheat flour

2 cups oat flour

¼ cup baking powder

½ Tbsp salt

3 ½ cups milk

1 lemon, juiced

Grated zest of 1 lemon

1 cup coconut oil, melted

3 large eggs, beaten

¼ cup honey

1 Tbsp ground flax seed + 3 Tbsp
  water, combined

Fruit and maple syrup, for serving

1. Preheat your waffle iron.

2. Stir together the dry ingredients (except the flax). In a separate bowl, whisk together the wet ingredients and the flax-water mixture.

3. In a large bowl, mix wet and dry ingredients together and stir until just combined. Don't over mix this—you still want a few tiny lumps here and there. Let rest for a few minutes while you clean up the kitchen.

4. Pour batter into your waffle maker according to manufacturer instructions (mine takes a scant ¼ cup); err on the side of adding less batter to avoid overflow. Cook until golden brown and crisp on the outside.

5. Remove cooked waffles. If you're eating them for breakfast right away, keep them in a warm oven on a baking sheet in a single layer (stacking will make them damp and limp). Top with fruit and maple syrup. (To meal prep, freeze extras. When ready to serve, microwave or toast the frozen waffles.)

Sunshine Waffles

These waffles will brighten your morning. The lemon gives them a lightness that will remind you of summer, and the whole grains and flax seed offer a nutritional punch that make you feel good about serving them to your family. And yes, this recipe makes A LOT of waffles, but you'll be stocking up your freezer. If you prefer, you can halve the recipe and just eat them fresh.

DAY 16
Much More

I'd always been warned about viewing God as a genie in a bottle, as if saying the right words in the right order guarantees an answered prayer. So for the longest time, I was careful to give God an easy way out, telling Him it's okay if He doesn't respond to my requests and sometimes even keeping my thoughts to myself because I didn't want to "bother" God with my pesky little asks.

Have you ever felt that way, even wondering if it's worth praying about something?

Does God really care about our struggle with yo-yo dieting?

Does He care that our medical bills are overdue?

Does He care that our hearts long for a real friend?

The Bible answers these questions with a resounding "yes!" In fact, Jesus compares our heavenly Father's heart with the heart of a parent who delights in his child's request for a loaf of bread. That dad wouldn't give his son a stone, right? Even the busiest of parents pause to feed their hungry child.

> *"If you, then, though you are evil, know how to give good gifts to your children, how much more will your Father in heaven give good gifts to those who ask him!" (Matt. 7:11)*

How much more?

It's a rhetorical question. Because the answer, of course, is SO MUCH MORE. More than we can even imagine. If on our worst days, we still take care of our children, imagine how much more our perfect heavenly Father loves to hear and meet our needs. He delights in giving us what is good.

This good Father wants to hear from you. Whatever is on your heart, no matter how big or small your request, ask Him. And keep asking. He'll never tire of your childlike faith as you trust Him to care for your every need.

> *"Ask and it will be given to you; seek and you will find; knock and the door will be opened to you." (Matt. 7:7)*

 Feast at the table | *If you have more time to linger at the breakfast table, open your Bible and let's FEAST on God's Word together!*

Focus on God

Open your Bible to Romans 10:11 and ask God to prepare your heart to receive His Word today.

Engage the Text

Read Matthew 7:7–11 out loud. This is a familiar text, so let's break it down here. List what Jesus tells His disciples to do in this passage.

What motivation does He give them to do this (first in verse 8 and then in verse 11)? How are these two reasons connected?

According to these verses, what roles do humility, action, and faith play in the believer's life?

In the Greek, ask, seek, and knock are present imperatives, which indicates a continuous action (i.e., "keep asking," "keep seeking," keep knocking"). What does that mean for the disciples' prayer lives?

How might a parent's perspective of "what is good" (verse 11) be different from a child's perspective? How might this higher understanding affect how the parent responds to the child's request?

What does the illustration in verses 9–10 reveal about the heart of God?

Assess the Main Idea

Some people wrongly interpret this text to mean that God is somehow obligated to give them whatever they ask for. Based on your observations above, is this an accurate interpretation? Why or why not?

What's the big idea of this passage? Write it in a short and succinct sentence.

Spark Transformation

How can you apply today's teaching in a small and measurable way in the next twenty-four hours?

Turn to God in Worship

What does this passage teach us about God's character? Take a few moments to worship Him for being a heavenly Father who gives good gifts, and most of all, the gift of His Spirit living in us (Luke 11:13).

PREP TIME: *20 minutes,*
plus 2 hours rest time

COOK TIME: *40 minutes*

YIELD: *8 servings*

❄ *Freezer-friendly*

✋ *Kid-friendly*

☑ *Meal Prep*

6 cups cubed day-old bread

1 ½ cups chopped cooked
turkey bacon

3 green onions, diced

1 handful spinach, sautéed
and chopped

2 cups shredded sharp
Cheddar cheese

10 large eggs

2 cups milk

½ tsp salt

½ tsp pepper

1. Spray 9x13-inch baking dish with cooking spray. Layer half the bread cubes in bottom of the dish. Layer bacon, veggies, and 1 ½ cups cheese, and top with remaining bread cubes.

2. In a large bowl, whisk together eggs, milk, salt, and pepper. Pour over bread mixture, pressing down slightly. Top with remaining ½ cup cheese.

3. Cover with aluminum foil and refrigerate at least 2 hours but no more than 12 hours. (To meal prep, prepare through step 3. When ready to bake, remove baking dish from fridge and allow to rest on the kitchen counter for 25–30 minutes. Move to step 4.)

4. Preheat oven to 350° F and bake until golden brown and the tip of a knife inserted in the center comes out clean, about 35 to 45 minutes.

5. Let stand 15 minutes before serving.

Overnight Eggy Breakfast Casserole

One gloomy January afternoon, I opened my fridge to realize I had a surplus of bread and eggs, and I realized I had the makings of a lazy Sunday morning breakfast. I threw in some green onion and spinach for a touch of green, but you can omit or swap out for other veggies of your choice. You can also cook this in the Crock-Pot, but you'll want to either grease the pot really well or use a Crock-Pot liner to make cleanup easy.

DAY 17
Recipe for Humble Love

 *Snack on the go*

If you're in a rush, the short devotional below is a quick "spiritual snack" to feed your soul and meditate on all day long.

If only she didn't do that. It always gets on my nerves! God, would You please change her? I can't stand it anymore!

Have you ever prayed something along those lines? I'll admit: I have. And I've often wondered why God didn't change the offending person.

In any relationship, there's bound to be conflict. But of course, we have no control over other people's actions. And although God *could* change other people, He often chooses to work on our own hearts instead.

We see this truth as Paul responds to the squabbles in the church in Philippi by pointing out the selfishness and conceit that drove them to hurt each other. And then, in a move that's classic Paul, he points them to Jesus as the ultimate example of humble love:

> *In your relationships with one another, have the same mindset as Christ Jesus:*
>
> > *Who, being in very nature God,*
> > > *did not consider equality with God something*
> > > > *to be used to his own advantage;*
> > *rather, he made himself nothing*
> > > *by taking the very nature of a servant,*
> > > *being made in human likeness.*
> > *And being found in appearance as a man,*
> > > *he humbled himself*
> > > *by becoming obedient to death—*
> > > > *even death on a cross! (Phil. 2:5–8)*

Talk about raising the bar! Paul redirects his readers' attention to the humility Jesus showed: the Creator-God let go of His glory and became the servant of those He created. Out of love.

This is the same attitude we are to exhibit toward one another, especially when we disagree.

What better training ground to learn humility and love than in difficult relationships? After all, these godly characteristics are not imparted through osmosis—they're learned in the fiery furnace of relational conflict.

Bring to mind the face of that person who's been annoying you, and instead of demanding that they change, ask God to change *you*. Ask Him to help you display the love and humility of Jesus in your next interaction.

Reread the passage above, and turn it into a prayer, asking God to make you a servant toward this person as you extend Jesus' love toward them.

 *Feast at the table* | *If you have more time to linger at the breakfast table, open your Bible and let's FEAST on God's Word together!*

Focus on God

Open your Bible to Deuteronomy 8:3 and ask Him to make you hunger for His Word more and more each day.

Engage the text

Read Philippians 2:5–11 out loud. Read it out loud again, slower this time. Did anything stand out to you? If so, write it down.

Now read it again, this time praying it out loud to Jesus, changing the pronoun references to second person (i.e., "You were in very nature God, and You did not consider equality with God something to be grasped, but made Yourself nothing . . .").

Go through and pray it one more time, out loud to Jesus, but this time pause after each statement and meditate on the truth you just spoke, writing down your notes in the space below. (For example, as you meditate on the phrase "You were in very nature God," consider what that means. Let your mind fill with the greatness of what it means that Jesus was God from everlasting.)

How have you experienced the implications of each statement in your own life? Take your time with this, allowing the truths of this text to move your heart, mind, soul, and spirit to gaze upon the beauty of Jesus Christ and to fill you with joy in His presence (Pss. 27:4; 16:11).

Respond to your worship experience in the space below. What was it like to engage the text in this way today?

What would it look like to have this attitude, as verse 5 exhorts?

Assess the Main Idea

Summarize the main idea of this passage in a sentence.

Spark Transformation

We cannot worship what we do not know. Consider learning about the nature of God by reading books like *Knowledge of the Holy* or *The Pursuit of God* by A. W. Tozer. Commit to deepening your understanding of and appreciation for God, whether by reading books on theology, singing theologically rich hymns, or listening to sermons that inspire a reverence and deeper love for God.

Turn to God in Worship

As you wrap up your time FEASTing on God's Word, continue your day's activities with the same spirit of worship, pausing to acknowledge Jesus' lordship over your life at stoplights, thanking Him for His sacrifice as you put dinner in the oven, and magnifying Him for His rule over the world as you lay your head on the pillow at night. Let all your words and deeds turn to God in worship today.

PREP TIME: *2 minutes*	COOK TIME: *2 minutes*	YIELD: *1 serving*

 Kid-friendly

½ cup whole milk

½ cup water

½ cup rolled oats

1 tsp maple syrup

2 Tbsp chopped pecans

Toppings: raspberries or other fruit, nuts, seeds, peanut butter, protein powder

1. Stir milk, water, and oats in a large microwavable bowl.

2. Microwave on high, pausing to stir every 30 seconds, until the mixture reaches the desired consistency. A shorter cooking time will result in a softer/runny oatmeal; a longer cooking time will make it firm up.

3. Top with chopped pecans, a drizzle of maple syrup, a splash of milk, or other toppings.

Microwavable Oatmeal Bowls

Some mornings you just want a quick but warm breakfast, and these microwavable oatmeal bowls are endlessly customizable. My favorite toppings are crushed pecans and a drizzle of maple syrup, but you can change it up with your favorite mix-ins. Unlike other recipes in this book, this makes a single serving and is cooked in the microwave. Feel free to multiply it by however many servings you need and cook on the stovetop if you prefer.

DAY 18
Sweeter than Honey

 Snack on the go

If you're in a rush, the short devotional below is a quick "spiritual snack" to feed your soul and meditate on all day long.

"Mommy, look!" My five-year-old called out as she pointed to the western sky. "Look at the sunset God painted tonight!"

The colors were indeed breathtaking. But my mommy heart melted to hear my child speak of God in such wondrous ways.

Motherhood has been the most humbling endeavor of my life. I make A LOT of mistakes in my parenting, but I'm grateful my children have learned at least this one thing from me: they see God's grandeur in His handiwork all around them. In fact, their little hearts are often more perceptive to His fingerprints than my own heart is.

The Bible tells us that all of creation points to its Creator: "The heavens declare the glory of God; the skies proclaim the work of his hands. Day after day they pour forth speech; night after night they reveal knowledge" (Ps. 19:1–2).

We can learn so much about our Creator if only we would pause long enough to recognize His fingerprints in the blade of grass and the bumble of bees.

> *What may be known about God is plain to them, because God has made it plain to them. For since the creation of the world God's invisible qualities— his eternal power and divine nature—have been clearly seen, being understood from what has been made, so that people are without excuse. (Rom. 1:19–20).*

This doesn't mean we toss out our Bibles because we can know everything we need to know about God simply by studying astronomy and botany. To the contrary, David goes on in Psalm 19 to exalt the virtues of God's self-revelation in Old Testament law, because it refreshes the soul, makes wise the simple, and is "sweeter than honey."

But we can also learn much by marveling at God's creativity in the world around us. Step outside into nature today. Listen to the rush of wind as it lifts your praises to Jesus. Study the intricate details in a single leaf that speak of an intelligent Designer. Smile at the birds' careless flight as our heavenly Father feeds them.

And join all creation in singing:
All creatures of our God and King,
Lift up your voice and with us sing,
O praise Him, Alleluia!

 Feast at the table | *If you have more time to linger at the breakfast table, open your Bible and let's FEAST on God's Word together!*

Focus on God

Open your Bible to Hebrews 1:3 and begin by asking God's Spirit to focus your heart and mind on Him as you read His Word.

Engage the Text

Read Psalm 19. If possible, go outside to look at the sky for a few moments. (Seriously, even if it's sweltering or freezing, you can do this for at least a minute. I promise you it's worth it.)

Read Psalm 19 again, speaking the words out loud as you allow their truths to sink deep into your heart. In what ways do the heavens and skies declare God's glory?

In the space below, create two columns for verses 7–11. In the first column, write out the description of the Lord's revealed law, and in the second, write out what happens when people read and obey the law.

What law was David referring to here? How does this law reveal God's glory?

What do verses 12–13 say about our ability to keep the law?

What does Paul add to this conversation in 2 Corinthians 3:7–18?

In other words, if the Old Testament law revealed God's glory (as Paul argues in the text above), in what way(s) does Jesus' work reveal something even more glorious?

How does David end his psalm?

Assess the Main Idea

Summarize the main idea of this passage in a single sentence.

Spark Transformation

As we saw today, both nature and Scripture speak of the majesty of God. How can you become a better "listener" to discern the beauty of God's glory as revealed in both?

Turn to God in Worship

Psalm 19:14 is a great verse to memorize and make your daily prayer. Take some time now to read it again, personalizing it with anything that's on your heart. Then step outside again and join the skies, the trees, and all of creation in praising God.

> *May these words of my mouth and this meditation of my heart*
> *be pleasing in your sight,*
> LORD, *my Rock and my Redeemer. (Ps. 19:14)*

✓ *Meal Prep*

6 cups milk

¹⁄₈ tsp salt

1 cup cream of wheat (also known as farina)

¹⁄₃ cup maple syrup (or to taste)

Toppings: fruit, nuts, seeds, maple syrup

1. In a medium saucepan, bring milk and salt to a low simmer. Keep a close eye on the milk so it doesn't boil over.

2. Gradually whisk in cream of wheat, stirring continuously until the mixture thickens (about 6 minutes) and bubbles.

3. Stir in maple syrup until well incorporated.

4. Immediately pour into bowls, careful not to burn yourself. If you let this sit in the saucepan, it will thicken and form a skin on top. This isn't a bad thing—it's just harder to dish out if you don't do it right away. (To meal prep, prepare through step 4. Store in an airtight container in the fridge for up to 5 days, and then reheat in the microwave.)

5. Top with your favorite toppings, like sliced bananas, sliced almonds, quartered strawberries, a spoonful of peanut butter, or a sprinkling of cocoa powder.

Creamy Cream of Wheat

Think of this as Cheesy Polenta's (p. 33) sweeter cousin: the perfect warm bowl to cuddle with under blankets on a bleak and dreary morning. I'll spoon this down as close to scalding hot as I can without burning my taste buds, and it feels like a giant hug in a bowl, from the inside out.

DAY 19
Full Plate

Are you overwhelmed?

Take a minute right now to download all your ideas, to-dos, and thoughts on a sticky note. Believe me, just getting it all on paper helps calm the chaos. . . .

. . . Wow. That's a lot, isn't it? I bet if you had more time, you could find even more things to write down. Whether little people are clamoring for clean underwear or coworkers are depending on us for that big project, we face more demands than we can handle. Think about that for a second: When the pressures threaten to overwhelm you, what do you do? How do you cope?

I often try to dig deeper and work harder. But the Bible has sobering words for us. In Psalm 127, Solomon offers this advice:

> *Unless the Lord builds the house,*
> *   the builders labor in vain.*
> *Unless the Lord watches over the city,*
> *   the guards stand watch in vain.*
> *In vain you rise early*
> *   and stay up late,*
> *toiling for food to eat—*
> *   for he grants sleep to those he loves. (Ps. 127:1–2)*

Our every breath is a gift from God. Our eyesight, our fingers and toes, our mental capacity . . . they're all gifts, undeserved, and often overlooked. Make no mistake, our success comes only by the grace of God. Sure, we can go to bed late and wake up early, but that will never be enough, will it? There will always be more to do than time to do it in.

Notice that in the verses above, builders and guards only succeed if the Lord is already at work. In other words, we need to join God in what He's doing, not expect Him to approve of what we're independently doing. God doesn't give us independent work—He invites us to work in dependence on Him, not independent of Him.

Go back to your list, and ask the Lord what things *He* has for you today, crossing everything else off. Those burdens are not yours to carry today.

As you check your mental or written list throughout the day, remind yourself that you're partnering with God in your work. It is He who is doing the work—He's just choosing to do it with and through you today. And that's a wonderfully light load to carry.

 Feast at the table | *If you have more time to linger at the breakfast table, open your Bible and let's FEAST on God's Word together!*

Focus on God

Open your Bible to Matthew 7:24, and write a prayer below asking God to help you build your life on His Word.

Engage the Text

Read Psalm 127 out loud.

This is a psalm of ascents. (Did you notice the little note right before verse 1?) This means that pilgrims would sing this song on their way to Jerusalem as they prepared to offer sacrifices at the temple. Read the psalm again, putting yourself in their shoes, imagining what would be on their minds and hearts as they sang this song.

As you read the lyrics, did you notice the two distinct but related themes in the two stanzas of the song? As you reread the psalm, where do you find a natural break?

Because the original text of this psalm was written in Hebrew, and most of us are reading a translation, we miss much of the poetry that would have been simple for the original hearers to understand. For example, the Hebrew word for "builders" in verse 1 is a pun on the word for "children" in verse 3. So the whole song is interconnected in beautiful ways, repeating the same theme in different situations.

As you reread this psalm, what do you think is the main theme of the first stanza (verses 1–2)?

What's the main theme of the second stanza (verses 3–5)?

How are the stanzas related? How are they different?

What does each stanza say about God's character? What about His gifts?

Assess the Main Idea

In one sentence, write out the main idea of the passage.

Spark Transformation

Choose one of the two stanzas and rewrite it in your own words using scenes from your own life to illustrate this psalm's truths.

Turn to God in Worship

End your Bible time by praising God for the ways He provides for His children, and specifically for the ways He's provided for you. Consider starting with the basics like food, shelter, health, family, and friends. Then move on to other gifts, like this week's paycheck, taste buds to enjoy this morning's breakfast, the beautiful colors of nature, the printing press that brought you this book (well, yeah! That's worth praising God for, right?), and so on.

PREP TIME: *3 minutes*　　　　**YIELD:** *4 servings*

⊘ *Gluten-free*

✋ *Kid-friendly*

☑ *Meal Prep*

---

1 cup water

2 oranges, peeled

3 cups fresh or frozen strawberries
  or raspberries

1 banana

1 cup Greek yogurt

1 cup ice cubes, optional

1. In a high-powered blender, blend water, fruit, and yogurt 30–45 seconds.

2. If using frozen fruit, omit ice. Otherwise, add ice cubes and blend an additional 30 seconds.

3. Pour into four glasses and enjoy!

To cut down on prep time and cleanup, assemble the fruit in the jars ahead of time and store in the fridge or freezer. Then blend the fruit with the other ingredients and pour back into the jars to enjoy!

Good Morning Smoothie

Sometimes I just want something pretty and pink for breakfast, and then I'll whip this up. You can use any berry you'd like: strawberries are sweeter but not as vibrantly pink as raspberries; blueberries turn this smoothie purple; cranberries will make it tart. But if you don't care about the color, throw in a handful of spinach for extra vitamins to energize you for your morning. And if you're a protein powder type of gal, feel free to add a scoop. Whatever way you make this, it'll be a delicious way to start your day.

DAY 20
Following the Light

 *Snack on the go* | *If you're in a rush, the short devotional below is a quick "spiritual snack" to feed your soul and meditate on all day long.*

Sunflowers have a special place in my heart. As a child, I used to wander through my grandfather's sunflower fields, smiling at the sunny yellow petals as I ran my finger around the circumference of the flower. Come fall, those same flowers would provide seeds for snacking and oil for cooking.

You probably already know that these flowers get their name from their curious ability to follow the sun. But did you know that they continuously readjust their position every 15–60 seconds?[17] That's slow enough to be imperceptible to the human eye, but fast enough to keep up with the sun's movement across the sky.

The spiritual parallels are unmistakable. Even though we're never called sunflowers in the Bible, Scripture often refers to Jesus as our Light.

Consider this introduction to Jesus from John's prologue: "In him was life, and that life was the light of all mankind. The light shines in the darkness, and the darkness has not overcome [or understood] it" (John 1:4–5).

When Jesus entered the world, He brought spiritual light to all who would turn to Him, but He didn't force anyone against their will. In this sense, those who lived in spiritual darkness did not understand Him, as we can see from His frequent encounters with unbelieving Jews who sought to kill Him. But others did seek to understand Him, and followed Him wherever He went, even to the cross (Mark 15:41).

I'm not trying to force a metaphor on Scripture, but I think we can be inspired by this beautiful portrayal of Jesus as the Light of the World . . . and the light that shines in our hearts:

> *For God, who said, "Let light shine out of darkness," made his light shine in our hearts to give us the light of the knowledge of God's glory displayed in the face of Christ. (2 Cor. 4:6)*

As we spend time with Jesus, His light will continue to shine in our hearts and also draw us into closer relationship with Him, a minute-by-minute readjustment of our position as we go about our daily work.

If you're the artistic type, consider drawing a sunflower and posting it somewhere you'll see it today. (If you're artistically challenged like me, perhaps you can print one out.) Whenever you see your sunflower, take a moment to readjust your heart toward the Light of the Son, tracking with Him throughout your day.

Feast at the table

If you have more time to linger at the breakfast table, open your Bible and let's FEAST on God's Word together!

Focus on God

Open your Bible to Psalm 119:114 and ask God to bring His Word to life in your life.

Engage the Text

Read John 1:1–18 out loud. Now read it again, slowing down to notice what words or images stand out to you.

In this passage, John uses the imagery of light and darkness to describe Jesus' entrance into the world. What does darkness signify?

Look up the meaning of the word "light" using an online Bible dictionary. What are some of the meanings?

In the physical world, what happens when light enters a dark room? How does this have spiritual parallels?

According to this passage, what does it mean that Jesus is light (see verses 12–18)?

Based on your knowledge of Jesus' life and ministry, in what ways was Jesus the Light of the World?

Read John 8:12 and 12:35–36. What additional insights do these passages offer about Jesus as light?

What else stands out to you in today's text?

Assess the Main Idea

Summarize the main idea of the passage in a single sentence.

Spark Transformation

According to Psalm 139:11–12, even darkness cannot be dark with God, because "darkness is as light to you." Underline this passage in your Bible.

Darkness threatens to overwhelm us when we allow sins to accumulate in our lives. Today, ask God's Spirit to shine His light in your heart and confess any sins that are hidden in darkness. End your prayer by thanking Jesus for His forgiveness and light in your life.

Turn to God in Worship

Thank God for sending Jesus as Light to the world. Consider listening to hymns and praise songs that center on this motif of Jesus as light. Here are a few suggestions:

"Shine, Jesus, Shine" (Graham Kendrick)
"Great Light of the World" (Bebo Norman)
"Lead, Kindly Light" (Audrey Assad)

You'll find wonderful songs on the playlist I curated for you at bibleandbreakfast.com.

Develop a Healthy Habit

Take a few moments to reflect on the past week and celebrate your progress. You may be surprised by what you learn, and you'll be more likely to be consistent in your new habit.

What have you learned about Jesus so far?

What are you enjoying about your *Bible and Breakfast* habit?

What's not working so well with your *Bible and Breakfast* habit, or what would you like to do differently?

What tweaks can you make to your morning time with Jesus to create a stronger and more enjoyable habit?

What would you like to say to Jesus as you reflect on the past week together? In the space below, write a few words of worship, praise, gratitude, or rededication.

PREP TIME: *2 minutes* | **COOK TIME:** *5 minutes*

 Kid-friendly

---

4 large eggs

4 slices of bread

4 slices of cheese

Butter

Salt and pepper

Fresh fruits, for serving

1. Using a cookie cutter or top of a glass, cut out a circle or other shape in the middle of the bread slices. Be careful not to cut into the crust.

2. Heat a griddle on medium-high heat. When hot, coat with cooking spray or butter. Carefully place the bread slices and cut-out shapes on the griddle to toast. Melt a small pat of butter in each circle.

3. Crack one egg into the center of each bread slice. Salt and pepper as desired. Using a spatula, move around the egg whites to cook more evenly, avoiding the yolk if you're going for a runny yolk.

4. When the egg white is fairly set, flip the bread and egg to cook on the other side, careful not to break the egg yolk. Top each with a slice of cheese, and cover with a pot lid to melt the cheese. Cook to desired doneness.

5. Plate each "egg in a basket," top with toasted circle, and serve with fruit of choice.

For holiday breakfasts, use different shapes of cookie cutters, like hearts for Valentine's Day or trees for Christmas.

Eggs in a Basket

I first heard of this twist on eggs and toast in college, when I was starry-eyed in love with my then-boyfriend and we'd meet up before sunrise to cook together in the college cafeteria. Ahh, what love does to unsuspecting youngsters. I'm happy to report we bonded over those breakfasts, and I'm still starry-eyed over that same man, and we still make eggs in a basket together (though thankfully not before sunrise). Nowadays, our kids love to help cut out the circles and layer the toppings over the eggs. We're passing on a life-changing breakfast recipe here, one I hope they carry with them into college and beyond.

DAY 21
Balanced

 *Snack on the go*

If you're in a rush, the short devotional below is a quick "spiritual snack" to feed your soul and meditate on all day long.

I was a sophomore in high school when this cute guy wanted to spend more time with me. But since I had solemnly sworn I wouldn't date until college, he had to get creative.

So he offered to teach me how to roller skate.

I'd always wanted to glide gracefully on skates, so I was eager to learn the basics. And he was eager to have an excuse to hold my hand. You know, to keep me from falling.

Skating requires a counterintuitive skill: you need to lean forward even when every fiber of your being wants to lean back to keep from falling flat on your face. So you focus your attention on this new skill, and when your concentration overrides your instinct, you experience the exhilaration of gliding over concrete. You practice this forward-leaning posture until it finally becomes second nature.

In many ways, our spiritual lives mirror learning this skill: we wobble through much of life leaning back on our own resources and wisdom because that gives us the illusion of control. But when we encounter bumps in the road, we quickly fall over.

Proverbs 3:5–6 puts it this way: "Trust in the LORD with all your heart and lean not on your own understanding; in all your ways submit to him, and he will make your paths straight."

We find freedom when we lean into the Lord. We were never meant to do this life on our own. From the beginning, God created us to lean into Him. It's the bumps and obstacles that remind us we need to cling tightly to Him.

I clung to that boy's hand as he whispered, "I've got you. Don't let go. Keep leaning forward. I've got you." Little did I know then that God would continue to use him through the tumultuous years to come, his hand holding mine as husband and wife, a picture of God's own pursuing and protective love.

Hear God's words spoken over you today: *I've got you. Don't let go. Keep leaning into Me. I will never let you go.*

What are those things weighing on your heart and mind today that you're trying to figure out? Write them out in the space below, and next to each one, write the words "I trust YOU, Lord."

Feast at the table

If you have more time to linger at the breakfast table, open your Bible and let's FEAST on God's Word together!

Focus on God

Open your Bible to Psalm 18:30 and ask God to help you read this passage with fresh eyes and to see His beauty in the text.

Engage the Text

Read Proverbs 3:5–6 out loud. These verses are often quoted for those facing big decisions, but sadly, they're often misquoted to imply that a simple prayer or two will secure God's blessing on whatever we decide. Today we're going to dig into these verses to better understand how God makes our paths straight and what that even means.

Write out Proverbs 3:5–6 in the space below.

What immediately stands out to you?

Number the three commands in these verses. How are all three related? How are they different?

Verse 5 contrasts trusting in the Lord with leaning on our own understanding. Is it possible to trust the Lord and depend on our own understanding at the same time? Why or why not?

Look up these verses in a few different translations. Write down what new words or phrases stand out to you or help you better understand this passage.

Using a Bible dictionary, look up the original Hebrew for the word "acknowledge." What does this word mean? How else is it used in other places in the Bible?

This word *yada`* is the same Hebrew word used for intimacy in marriage. How does this illuminate the meaning of the word translated above? What does it mean to "acknowledge" God in all our ways?

What does the writer say God will do when we trust Him, lean on Him, and acknowledge Him?

What "paths" do you think the writer is referring to here?

Can you think of any people in the Bible who lived out this passage and were surprised by the way God directed their paths? How do their examples illustrate the truth of this proverb?

Assess the Main Idea

Summarize the main idea of the passage in a single sentence.

Spark Transformation

Is there a situation in your life that you need to entrust to God? In what ways can you acknowledge Him in your daily activities?

Turn to God in Worship

This Proverb encourages us to seek a personal, intimate relationship with God, getting to know Him deeply in everything we do each day. It's thrilling and humbling to think that the Creator of the world would invite us to know Him on such a deep level. Take time today not just to thank Him for this privilege, but also to draw near to Him, quieting your heart and mind to simply enjoy His presence and asking Him for a deepening relationship with Him.

⊘ *Gluten-free*

✋ *Kid-friendly*

☑ *Meal Prep*

---

6 cups rolled oats

2 cups chopped walnuts, almonds, or pecans

1/3 cup good-quality cocoa powder

1/4 tsp cinnamon

1/4 tsp salt

2/3 cup coconut oil, melted

1/2 cup honey or maple syrup

1 Tbsp vanilla extract

1 cup mini chocolate chips (you can also chop a sugar-free chocolate bar if you prefer)

1 cup coconut flakes

1 1/2 cups unsweetened dried fruit

Fresh fruit, nuts, yogurt, for serving

1. Grease interior of Crock-Pot with coconut oil. Stir together dry ingredients directly into the pot.

2. In a small bowl, mix together coconut oil, honey or maple syrup, and vanilla extract. Stir into oat mixture until well blended. *Don't add the chocolate chips, coconut flakes, or dried fruit yet.*

2. Cover and cook on high for 45 minutes to 2 hours, leaving the lid slightly vented. Stir every 15 minutes. You can cook it as little as 45 minutes for a softer granola, or up to 2 hours if you like yours golden and crunchy like we do. Alternatively, bake in the oven at 300° F to desired crunchiness, about 30–45 minutes, stirring every 10 minutes. Add chocolate chips and dried fruit in the last 10 minutes.

3. In the last 15 minutes, stir in the chocolate chips, coconut flakes, and dried fruit. Smile big when you see the chocolate melt and create granola clusters. Obligatory taste test.

4. Spread the granola on a baking sheet and let it cool before transferring to an airtight container. Enjoy!

Chocolate Triple Nut Granola

Chocolate for breakfast? Yes, please! This yummy chocolate granola is filled with good-for-you fats courtesy of the nuts and coconut oil that will help you feel full longer. I like layering Greek yogurt with freshly sliced strawberries and sprinkling it with this gluten-free chocolate granola. I'm pretty sure this will be on the menu at the marriage supper of the Lamb. Or maybe breakfast the day after.

DAY 22
Salty

I'm so grateful for modern conveniences like refrigerators and freezers. Aside from the delicious food I can meal prep and freeze for busy days (like those yummy breakfast burritos on page 102 and morning glory muffins on page 171), I'm grateful to have so many convenience foods at my fingertips.

But in the ancient world, before electricity, people preserved their meats by rubbing in salt. More than just a condiment, salt slowed down decay and kept foods fresh longer.

This brings new meaning to the passage where Jesus tells His disciples: "You are the salt of the earth" (Matt. 5:13). In other words, Jesus' followers in society could slow down moral decay by their very presence.

This world is evil. Just read the headlines in today's paper, and you'll find enough bad news to keep you awake all night. But that's nothing new. The powerful have always preyed on the weak, and God has always called His people to stand against evil:

> "*Learn to do right; seek justice.*
> *Defend the oppressed.*
> *Take up the cause of the fatherless;*
> *plead the case of the widow.*"
> (Isa. 1:17)

While we may feel overwhelmed by the needs of the whole wide world, God's Spirit compels us to do something—to step in, to love, and to rescue. We are strategically placed to be salt and light to those around us.

Picture the faces of the people God has placed in your life this year: your neighbors, your kids' teachers, your favorite barista. How might God want to use you right where you are? Write a few ideas in the space below.

Now pick one way you can be God's salt on the earth in the next few days. Ask God to empower you to do the next right thing, and then take out your salt shaker and place it in a conspicuous spot to remind you to take action.

Then, once you've done the thing God is calling you to do, come back to this page and write out what happened, as a way of remembering God's faithfulness in our daily acts of obedience.

 Feast at the table | *If you have more time to linger at the breakfast table, open your Bible and let's FEAST on God's Word together!*

Focus on God

Open your Bible to Luke 11:28 and write a prayer below, asking God's Spirit to quiet your heart and mind in Him so that you may hear God's Word and obey it today.

Engage the Text

Read Isaiah 1:1–20 out loud. This passage is not one we hear often, so let's slow down and read it again. Underline words or phrases that jump out at you.

Take a closer look at verses 1–9. What do these verses say about the state of Israel?

Describe the comparison Isaiah makes in verses 3–4. What does this say about the condition of the hearts of the people?

Look at verses 6–8 again; how does Isaiah describe the current state of Israel?

According to verses 2 and 5, what led to this situation?

Let's dig a bit deeper to better understand exactly what Israel was doing that was so displeasing to God. Read the related passage in 2 Chronicles 28:1–4 and list the sins of the Israelites. (Don't skip this—it really helps you understand the gravity of the situation Isaiah is preaching against.)

What did God do because of their sin (see 2 Chronicles 28:5 and Isaiah 1:7–8)? According to Isaiah 1:11–15, what did God think of the Israelites' religious activities?

Although God would have been justified in wiping out the entire population of Israel, what does He do in verse 9? What does that say about God's character?

What do the imperatives in verses 16–17 reveal about what's important to God?

This passage pivots in verse 18. Write out the verse in the space below.

What is shocking about the tone of this verse?

What attributes of God does it reveal?

This book is also filled with promises and prophesies, including some of the most beautiful descriptions of the Messiah who would come to save His people. Skip ahead to Isaiah 30:15–17. How does this passage reaffirm the truths of today's text but also add to it?

What do today's passages teach us about God's character?

Assess the Main Idea

That's a lot of ground we just covered. Summarize the main idea of this passage in a sentence.

Spark Transformation

What did God want from the Israelites? From His children?

According to Romans 12:1, what sacrifice does God want from us today?

How does this relate to Isaiah 1:16–17 in your own life?

Turn to God in Worship

Read Isaiah 53:4–5, where Isaiah describes the Suffering Servant who would save His people (that is, Jesus). What similarities do you see between this passage and Isaiah 1:5–6?

How does Isaiah 53 relate to the forgiveness spoken of in Isaiah 1:18? What does this say about the love of God and the mission of Jesus? Throughout the day, thank God for the gifts of forgiveness and salvation.

⊘ *Gluten-free*
✋ *Kid-friendly*

4 cups spring mix
1 large tomato, cut into wedges
6 pieces bacon, cooked and chopped
1 avocado, pitted and thinly sliced
2 large eggs
Optional toppings: greens (spinach, kale, arugula); protein (leftover grilled chicken); satisfying fats (goat cheese, mozzarella); crunch (shredded carrot, nuts, seeds, croutons); extras (leftover roasted veggies, balsamic glaze)

1. Cook bacon to desired crispiness. Remove to paper-towel-lined covered plate and let cool. Then chop.

2. Soft boil your eggs (six minutes in boiling water is perfect for me). Peel and set aside.

3. Layer lettuce, bacon, and tomato on two plates. Top with avocado slices.

4. Cut open soft-boiled egg on top of salad. The yolk runs over the greens, so I find I don't need additional dressing.

5. Add any additional toppings you'd like!

BLT Breakfast Salad

As you can tell, I take my breakfasts (and my Bible) very seriously. It's my favorite meal of the day, but it's also easy to get stuck in a rut. One year, I was trying out this weird elimination diet that had me eating salad for breakfast. I know, I know, that sounds wrong. But I found out there's a science to eating salad for breakfast, and even though I quit that bizarre diet (and dieting in general), salads have remained a regular in my breakfast rotation. This isn't so much a recipe as it is a formula for making your own variation of breakfast salads.

DAY 23
Intentional Hospitality

 *If you're in a rush, the short devotional below is a quick "spiritual snack" to feed your soul and meditate on all day long.*

The Bible is filled with fascinating stories of discipleship happening around the table.

In Acts 18, we're introduced to a husband and wife team named Aquila and Priscilla. They had moved hundreds of miles from their home in Rome as the emperor had expelled all the Jews. Yet even in exile, they welcomed people around their table, including a traveling preacher named Paul. They quickly became friends, bonding over their common trade of tent making, and they invited Paul to move in with them

These three ate, worked, and talked about Jesus together. They probably chatted about ordinary things like the price of leather and the increase in taxes. But they also journeyed together, preaching about Jesus in one city after another until they reached Ephesus. There, Priscilla and Aquila remained to disciple new believers while Paul continued his missionary journey.

Soon after, a man named Apollos came to town, speaking eloquently and enthusiastically about Jesus. But as Aquila and Priscilla listened to him preach, they realized he didn't know the whole story. So they took him aside and shared what they had learned from Paul (see Acts 18:24–26).

I imagine Priscilla sat Apollos at Paul's former place at the table and, together with her husband, explained the beautiful gospel they had learned from their conversations with Paul. Apollos humbly accepted their correction, embraced Jesus' salvation, and continued his missionary journey with renewed zeal, helping believers wherever he traveled (Acts 18:27–28).

Great kingdom impact often starts in tiny gestures of hospitality around our tables. While Priscilla and Aquila remained in Ephesus, their hospitality created ripple effects throughout the ancient world, wherever Paul and Apollos traveled. Here's what Paul writes to the church in Corinth, where he had spent almost two years in Priscilla and Aquila's home:

"We each carried out our servant assignment. I planted the seed, Apollos watered the plants, but

God made you grow. It's not the one who plants or the one who waters who is at the center of this process but God, who makes things grow" (1 Cor. 3:6–7 MSG).

How might God use your intentional hospitality to change someone else's life? Invite one person to join you for breakfast or coffee this week, and find out.

 *Feast at the table* | *If you have more time to linger at the breakfast table, open your Bible and let's FEAST on God's Word together!*

Focus on God

Open your Bible to Job 23:12 and begin by asking the Lord to help you treasure His Word more than your favorite food.

Engage the Text

Read Acts 18 out loud. Write down the main characters in this chapter, and note one observation about each of them.

Why were Aquila and Priscilla in Corinth (see verse 2)?

Based on verses 1–3, what was Paul's relationship with Aquila and Priscilla?

What were their daily activities (see verses 3–4)?

What was their main topic of conversation (see verse 5)?

How did the couple aid Paul in his proclamation of the gospel (see verses 18–19)?

Did Paul help them? If so, how?

What were some of the hardships Paul encountered in Corinth? What was Paul's emotional state, as described by the Lord in his vision (verses 9–10)?

How might Aquila and Priscilla's hospitality have aided Paul during the hardships he endured in Corinth?

Was this a short-term or long-term arrangement (see verses 11 and 18)? What would be some challenges of such a living arrangement?

Who else did this couple take into their home, according to verses 24–26? How is this similar to the hospitality shown to Paul? How is it different?

How do hospitality and discipleship go together, according to the example in this chapter?

What are the ripple effects of Priscilla and Aquila's investment in Apollos, according to verses 27–28?

What else stands out to you as you study this passage?

Assess the Main Idea

In a single sentence, summarize the main idea of this passage. Try to make it precise, concise, and memorable.

Spark Transformation

Acts 18 clearly models a pattern of discipleship, as Paul pours into Priscilla and Aquila, and they in turn invest in Apollos, who goes on to preach and disciple others through his travels. Priscilla and Aquila model daily discipleship around the table, serving both physically and spiritually.

Who has God placed in your life right now for the purpose of discipleship?

Ask the Holy Spirit to show you opportunities to disciple others, starting with those in your own family. What's one practical way you can show hospitality to someone in your life this week?

Turn to God in Worship

Though Paul, Priscilla, Aquila, and Apollos seem to be the main characters of this passage, the bigger character empowering them is God. According to Ephesians 2:10, what do these believers' actions say about God?

The Greek word for "workmanship" sometimes has the connotation of a "work of art." What does this say about God?

Spend some time worshiping God for who He is and how He works in the world, not only in Paul's days but in our lifetime as well.

⊘ *Gluten-free*
☑ *Meal Prep*

---

1 large sweet potato, peeled and chopped (about 2 cups)

1/2 cup chopped onion

1/2 cup chopped red bell pepper

1/2 cup chopped yellow bell pepper

1 small zucchini, chopped

2 garlic cloves, minced

1 cup quartered mushrooms

1/2 cup bite-sized pieces bacon

4 large eggs

Salt and pepper to taste

1/4 cup shredded Cheddar cheese

Handful of parsley, chopped (optional)

1. Preheat the oven to 425° F. After you've cleaned and chopped the veggies, transfer to a sheet pan, drizzle lightly with olive oil, and toss to coat. Arrange bacon pieces on top. (To meal prep, clean and chop the veggies and store in an airtight container in the fridge until ready to roast.)

2. Roast the veggies until the sweet potatoes are fork tender yet still firm, about 15–18 minutes.

3. Remove the sheet pan from the oven and stir veggies with a wooden spoon. With the back of the spoon, make 4 indentations into the hash. Crack an egg into each of the indentations, sprinkling with salt and pepper. Return to the oven and bake to desired doneness, 4 minutes for runny yolks to 8 minutes for firm yolks.

4. Top with a sprinkling of cheese and allow to melt before serving. Garnish with chopped parsley, if using.

Sheet Pan Healthy Morning Hash

There are mornings when I want something simple, and there are mornings when I want something satisfying. And then some mornings, I want both. This recipe fits the bill. I love that it's adaptable so I can use whatever breakfast meat and veggies I have on hand, and because it's baked in the oven, I can read my Bible while it cooks.

DAY 24
Straining and Pressing

 Snack on the go

We all have things in our past we'd rather forget.

Sins. Regrets. Mistakes.

And our enemy often dredges up the past to tell us we're frauds. We're unlovable. We're hopeless. That's what he wants us to think.

Take a moment to identify which parts of your past haunt you. What feelings are associated with those memories? How do they affect your identity or how you relate to God?

If we allowed the voice of our enemy to condemn us, our past could easily define us, overwhelm us, and even paralyze us. But we serve a God who heals our brokenness and then uses those very things that would disqualify us to bring hope and healing to others.

If anyone understood this, it was Paul. He had once been a religious big shot, but in his blind zeal he became a murderer and terrorist. But God's grace saved him, changed him, and placed him on a new trajectory.

Paul could have been debilitated by his past mistakes, but he chose instead to focus on one thing alone: "Forgetting what is behind and straining toward what is ahead, I press on toward the goal to win the prize for which God has called me heavenward in Christ Jesus" (Phil. 3:13b–14).

Paul refused to be defined by his past. Like Paul, we can choose to fix our attention on Jesus: knowing Him more, emulating Him more, and growing closer to Him.

Is there something you need to let go of or confess to Jesus? Open your hands in front of you and picture yourself holding in your palms those sins, regrets, and mistakes that haunt you.

Then imagine Jesus extending His own hands toward you, the marks of the nails still visible in His palms. All your past is covered by His blood shed on that cross. There is nothing that's too horrible for Him to forgive.

Now pray these words adapted from Micah 7:19:

> You will again have compassion on [me]; you will tread [my] sins underfoot and hurl all [my] iniquities into the depths of the sea.

 Feast at the table

If you have more time to linger at the breakfast table, open your Bible and let's FEAST on God's Word together!

Focus on God

Open your Bible to Psalm 19:7 and ask the Spirit to focus your heart and mind on Him, and to give you clarity of thought as you study Scripture.

Engage the Text

Read Philippians 3:12–16 out loud. Read it again slowly, starting with verse 1 to understand the context and pausing to notice the details.

Write down your observations on the text. What immediately jumps out to you?

What is the "this" Paul refers to in verse 12? (See the preceding verses for context.)

What phrase is repeated three times in the first two verses? What does this phrase mean?

How does focusing on "what's behind" stand in contrast with Paul's desire to "press on" (verses 12 and 14)?

What imagery does Paul use to describe the Christian life?

How does 1 Corinthians 9:24–27 further clarify this metaphor?

What is the "one thing" Paul does (see verse 13)?

What does Paul "forget"? How does he do this?

What is ahead and how does Paul "strain" for it?

What is the "prize" of the Christian race (see verses 10–11)?

If you'd like to go deeper, pick one of the key words or phrases in this passage and do a word study to understand how it's used throughout Scripture. How do these layers of meaning add to your understanding of today's passage?

Assess the Main Idea

In one sentence, summarize the main idea of this passage.

Spark Transformation

The "one thing" Paul strained toward was not merely factual knowledge about Jesus, but also experiential knowledge—living in the power of His resurrection and fellowship in His suffering and likeness in His death.

How does one gain this *experiential knowledge*? In what ways have you experienced Jesus personally?

Turn to God in Worship

Today, use the REST method to respond to God's Word in prayer.

Recite God's goodness: Praise God for something you learned about Him in today's passage.

Express your neediness: Is there something you need to confess to Him?

Seek His stillness: Pause for a few moments to simply be still with God. Listen to Him in the silence.

Trust His faithfulness: What area(s) of your life do you need to surrender and entrust to God's loving care today?

❄ *Freezer-friendly*

✋ *Kid-friendly*

☑ *Meal Prep*

———————

3 cups peeled and grated carrots

2 cups grated zucchini (I leave the peel on for the vibrant green color)

3 small ripe bananas, mashed

4 large eggs

1/2 cup turbinado sugar

1/2 cup honey

1/2 cup + 1 Tbsp melted coconut oil

2 1/2 tsp vanilla extract

2 cups all-purpose flour

1 cup whole wheat pastry flour

2 1/2 tsp cinnamon

2 1/4 tsp baking soda

3/4 tsp baking powder

1/2 tsp salt

1/2 cup walnuts, chopped, plus extra for topping

1. Gently toss together carrots, zucchini, and bananas in a large bowl. Make a well in the center.

2. In the center well, stir together eggs, sugar, honey, oil, and vanilla extract until homogenous. Gently fold prepped veggies and banana to incorporate it all together.

3. In a large bowl, stir together dry ingredients (not including the walnuts). Make a well in the center, and add the wet ingredients, stirring just enough to moisten the dry mixture (12 to 15 circular stirs with a spoon should be enough). Gently fold in the walnuts just until combined. Batter should be lumpy but not have any areas of dry flour.

4. Marvel at the beautiful colors and textures, and try really hard not to eat this with a spoon. It's like carrot cake meets zucchini bread meets cinnamon muffins. Not that I would know . . .

5. Pour batter into greased muffin tins until 3/4 full. Sprinkle with extra walnuts. Preheat oven to 400° F. Bake for 8 minutes and then lower temperature to 350° F until a toothpick inserted in the center comes out clean, about 10 minutes longer. Let muffins cool in the tin for 10 minutes, and then transfer to a wire rack to cool completely. Store in airtight container in the fridge for 3 to 5 days.

Morning Glory Muffins

These nutritional powerhouse muffins will make you proud to be eating veggies for breakfast without sacrificing any flavor or texture. Other morning glory muffins might feature raisins and coconut, but I've swapped those out for other ingredients my family prefers. My kids and I will sometimes bake these in mini-muffin tins to give to neighbors and new moms. The small muffins will finish baking sooner, so watch them closely.

DAY 25
Enough

 Snack on the go

If you're in a rush, the short devotional below is a quick "spiritual snack" to feed your soul and meditate on all day long.

Imagine what your life would look like if you had access to a debit card that was refilled each morning with a million dollars. Nothing carries over to the next day—but you can use as much as you want each day. How would this inheritance change your spending habits? Do you think it would make you more content?

While I don't have a magical debit card to give you, Scripture tells us we have something even better. In Ephesians 1:3 Paul says:

> *Praise be to the God and Father of our Lord Jesus Christ, who has blessed us in the heavenly realms with every spiritual blessing in Christ.*

Did you catch that? God blessed us with *every* spiritual blessing in the heavenly realms.

Every blessing. Nothing held back.

There's nothing you need today that you don't already have in Jesus.

Peace? It's yours in Christ.

Joy? Already yours in Jesus.

Love? Patience? Self-control? Kindness? Life eternal?

Yes, yes, yes, yes, and yes. Everything you need you already have in Jesus. But how often do we go about our day as spiritual orphans, living in spiritual poverty, begging God for riches He's already granted us?

He's holding nothing back, friend. If you belong to Jesus, you have everything you need and more than you could ever want—a heavenly inheritance beyond your wildest dreams.

What does your soul need today? Write it in the space below. Thank God for already providing it for you, along with the abundance of spiritual blessings that are yours in Christ.

Better than a loaded debit card, God's blessings satisfy our souls' deepest longings. You and I have Jesus. And He is enough.[18]

 *Feast at the table* | *If you have more time to linger at the breakfast table, open your Bible and let's FEAST on God's Word together!*

Focus on God

Open your Bible to Proverbs 4:20–21 and rewrite the verses into a prayer, asking God's Spirit to remove any distraction and help you focus on Him.

Engage the Text

Read Ephesians 1:7–14 out loud. Back up and read the passage again, beginning with verse 1.

Write down any observations that immediately stand out to you.

Paul begins his letter to the believers in Ephesus by assuring them of their spiritual inheritance. What does verse 3 say about God's generosity? About a believer's inheritance?

Verse 7 reminds readers that redemption comes through Jesus. The Ephesians would have been familiar with the ancient practice of freeing a slave by paying a ransom price. How does this imagery explain the spiritual redemption Jesus made available to us?

The phrase "in Him" or "in Christ" appears eight times in these eight verses (and twelve times in the whole chapter). Circle each occurrence in your Bible, and then list as many as you can in the space below, noting what Paul says is found in Christ each time.

One of the spiritual blessings Paul describes in verse 11 is being "chosen" in Jesus Christ. What does this mean?

According to the passage, what does it mean to be "in Christ"?

The three persons of the Trinity appear (directly or indirectly) in this passage. What does the text say about each of them?

Another phrase that's repeated twice in this passage is "to the praise of His glory" (also in verse 6). What is to God's praise? What does that say about the Christian life?

What does this passage teach about believers' lives?

What else stands out to you in this passage?

Assess the Main Idea

Write out the main idea of this passage in a single sentence. Make it precise, concise, and memorable.

Spark Transformation

If you are a believer in Jesus Christ, everything Paul writes in this passage to the Ephesians is true of you too. Go back and reread what is yours "in Christ." Which of these phrases stands out to you the most today? Why do you think that is?

What would it look like for you to live out the reality of your spiritual blessing in Christ? Today, specifically, how can your behavior reflect the one characteristic that stood out to you most?

Turn to God in Worship

There's so much richness in today's passage about God's character. Pick out a few attributes and spend time praising God for who He is and all He has done.

What stood out to you in today's Bible and Breakfast? Share on social media and tag me @asheritah and #bibleandbreakfast!

PREP TIME: *10 minutes* | COOK TIME: *20 minutes* | YIELD: *20 energy bites*

❄️ *Freezer-friendly*

⊘ *Gluten-free*

✋ *Kid-friendly*

☑️ *Meal Prep*

---

1 cup rolled oats

¼ cup ground flaxseed

⅔ cup unsweetened coconut
   flakes, toasted

½ cup almond butter

⅓ cup honey

¼ cup unsweetened cocoa powder

1 Tbsp chia seeds

1 tsp vanilla extract

1. Stir all ingredients together in a medium bowl until thoroughly mixed. If the mixture seems too dry, stir in an extra tablespoon of almond butter. If it seems too wet, try adding extra oats.

2. Cover and chill in the fridge for 20–30 minutes.

3. Use a spoon to scoop out the mixture and roll into 1-inch balls.

4. Store in an airtight container for up to two weeks, or in the freezer for even longer.

Marathon Chocolate Energy Bites

I first made these energy bites after experimenting with the Sugarfast Power Balls (p. 83). My husband was training for a half marathon and grabbed these to fuel up on his morning run. He said they gave him an instant boost of energy and told me not to change the recipe. So now they have a permanent place in my breakfast repertoire, and I try to keep some in the fridge even for mornings when the only marathon I run is running errands.

DAY 26
Paul Tested, God-Approved

 *Snack on the go* | *If you're in a rush, the short devotional below is a quick "spiritual snack" to feed your soul and meditate on all day long.*

I'm embarrassed to admit that I've not always shown loving hospitality.

I've served meals begrudgingly.

I've avoided eye contact while refilling water glasses.

I've retreated to the kitchen so I wouldn't have to endure small talk.

And each time, God's Spirit has convicted me that I've opened my home but not my heart. You see, it's easier to talk about God's love than it is to live it out, especially toward people who hurt us. And sometimes those hurts carry over into new relationships, making us hesitant to invite again, open the door again, and love again. It just seems too risky—too hard.

But it's in the hard places that God softens our hearts.

Paul knew all about this. On one of his missionary journeys to Philippi, he was wrongly accused and mistreated, suffering at the hands of those he was hoping to reach with the good news of Jesus. But Paul saw these hardships as God's way of purifying his motivations, stripping him of any people-pleasing or selfish ambitions.

At the risk of being misunderstood and rejected, Paul continued to pursue relationships:

> *Just as a nursing mother cares for her children, so we cared for you. Because we loved you so much, we were delighted to share with you not only the gospel of God but our lives as well. (1 Thess. 2:7b–8)*

You see, the gospel was always meant to be poured out into relationships, not contained inside a building. And yes, that's going to cost us. Just like a new mom sacrifices sleep and personal space and a million other things to care for her little baby, so we are called to love those around us with the love of Jesus, even when it costs us our own personal comforts.

Who is God calling you to show that kind of love toward this week? Consider calling to invite her over for brunch, and ask God to empower you to share your hope and heart with her.

 *Feast at the table*

If you have more time to linger at the breakfast table, open your Bible and let's FEAST on God's Word together!

Focus on God

Open your Bible to Proverbs 4:5, asking God's Spirit to fill you with all wisdom and understanding as you focus your heart and mind on Him.

Engage the Text

Read 1 Thessalonians 2:1–12 out loud. Now read it again, writing down any observations that come to mind as you read.

According to verses 1–2, what personal costs did Paul and his companions face while preaching the good news of Jesus?

What motivated them to push through the hardships (verses 3–4 and 8)?

Paul uses two similes in this passage to explain his behavior toward this young church. What are they? (Hint: see verses 7 and 11.)

What do each reveal about his affection and attitude toward the young believers in Thessalonica?

According to this passage, what was Paul's message (verse 12)?

What does Paul describe as his purpose while living among this young church, in verse 8?

What were some of his concerns in carrying out his calling?

What method did he use to fulfill his calling?

What attribute of God does Paul appeal to in verses 5 and 10? How does this characteristic of God affect Paul's life?

Assess the Main Idea

Write out the main idea of this passage in a single sentence. Make it precise, concise, and memorable.

Spark Transformation

Paul says his main concern was to share the gospel and live it out among the Thessalonians. Can you accurately and succinctly explain the gospel to someone who is unfamiliar with Jesus Christ?

Today, find a trusted friend or family member and try telling them what God has done in your life in ninety seconds or less. Continue sharing this good news of who Jesus is and what He has done, and pray that you may be prepared to "speak as [a woman] approved by God to be entrusted with the gospel" (2:4).

Turn to God in Worship

Several times in this passage, Paul points to God as his witness regarding his sincerity in sharing the gospel. Yet there is no undertone of fear or guilt, but rather one of sincerity and peace. How does God's omniscience (He knows everything) and omnipresence (He is everywhere) make you feel?

Read Psalm 139 and make it your prayer, worshiping God for His love that covers all our failings.

If you need help articulating the gospel message, go to onethingalone.com/salvation for a helpful guide.

| **PREP TIME:** 5 *minutes* | **COOK TIME:** 5 *minutes* | **YIELD:** 4 *servings* |

❄ *Freezer-friendly*
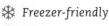 *Kid-friendly*

---

4 uncooked breakfast sausage patties

4 English muffins (you can also use biscuits or bagels)

1 Tbsp butter

4 large eggs

4 slices Cheddar cheese

Fresh spinach leaves and tomato slices, optional

1. In a large frying pan, cook sausage patties over medium-high heat until no longer pink. Set aside on a paper towel to drain.

2. Meanwhile, toast English muffins.

3. Wipe frying pan clean and return to heat. Melt butter and crack in eggs, cooking to desired doneness. Top with cheese while egg is still cooking to achieve maximum meltiness.

4. Arrange a sausage patty and an egg and cheese on the bottom half of a muffin, followed by the top. Assemble the remaining sandwiches the same way. For extra color and texture, add a few spinach leaves on the bottom of the English muffin before adding the sausage.

5. Serve immediately, with tomato slices, if desired. Or, if you'd like to freeze them, let cool completely before wrapping in a paper towel and aluminum foil. To reheat, remove foil and microwave frozen Easy Breakfast sandwich on medium-low for 2–3 minutes or until thoroughly reheated, flipping halfway through cooking time.

Easy Breakfast Sandwich

I don't have many guilty pleasures in life, but breakfast sandwiches from a certain golden-arched fast food restaurant would come close. The good news is that I can easily recreate these at home, which gives me better control over the ingredients and turns these into guilt-free sandwiches.

DAY 27
Lovingly Serve

 **Snack on the go** | *If you're in a rush, the short devotional below is a quick "spiritual snack" to feed your soul and meditate on all day long.*

It's easy to extend niceties toward someone without actually opening our heart to them. It's easy to say we love people—it's a lot harder to live it out, especially when they're hard to love.

The apostle John understood this all too well. Known as "the apostle Jesus loved," John experienced the extravagance of Jesus' love firsthand and wrote extensively on the subject in his epistles. But like the rest of us, John learned to love the hard way.

In an almost comical scene in Scripture, John and James ask Jesus to give them prominent places in the new government they were sure He would institute when He overthrew the Romans. *Never mind these other ten guys,* is the implication. *Give us the best spots!*

This audacious request came just after Jesus revealed that He would suffer and die, and all these two brothers could think about was themselves. When the other disciples heard what happened, they were indignant. In fact, Scripture records that they got into an argument about who was the greatest, and Jesus reminded them of His call to lay down their lives for one another. (For the whole story, see Mark 10:32–45.)

It's perhaps with this backstory in mind that John wrote to the early churches, "This is how we know what love is: Jesus Christ laid down his life for us. And we ought to lay down our lives for our brothers and sisters" (1 John 3:16). John learned this lesson the hard way, and he was eager for early believers to learn and live this out as well, as he continues: "let us not love with words or speech but with actions and in truth" (1 John 3:18).

We can stop trying to promote ourselves, seeking instead to lovingly serve those God places in our lives. Let's not just talk about love. Let's live it out.

When the kids "help" with pancakes but make a bigger mess, love them.

When the person who hurt you walks by in the church hallway, love them.

When you're tempted to recount all your spouse's past shortcomings, love them.

Loving people gets harder the closer we get to them, because opening your heart means opening yourself to the risk of hurt.

Our families and neighbors will see Jesus' love in us not in what we say but in what we do. May we be women who love well.

 *Feast at the table* | *If you have more time to linger at the breakfast table, open your Bible and let's FEAST on God's Word together!*

Focus on God

Open your Bible to 1 Peter 1:23, asking God to help you encounter the living Word of God in the pages of Scripture.

Engage the Text

Read 1 John 3:11–20 out loud. Write your observations below.

This letter is written by the apostle John, author of the gospel of John, the epistles of John, and Revelation. According to John 13:23, how does John describe himself?

If you have a study Bible, read the notes on the author (if not, you can find notes online by searching BlueLetterBible.com or a similar Bible study site).

How does knowing who wrote this passage inform our understanding of this text?

According to verse 11, what is the message John preached from the beginning?

A quick skim through this letter reveals that love is the main theme. Count how many times the word "love" appears in today's passage, then list what you learn about sincere love from each occurrence in the text.

According to verse 16, how do believers know what love is?

How does Jesus' example propel believers to sincere love?

According to Jesus' words recorded in John 13:35, what is the significance of love in the believer's life?

What does that love look like practically (see 1 John 3:17–18)?

How do actions relate to feelings in the believer's life, according to today's text?

What provides the assurance of salvation in a believer's life if there is any doubt?

If you'd like to go deeper, check a few cross-references and write down what these additional passages add to your understanding of Christian love.

What do you learn about God in today's texts?

Assess the Main Idea

Write out the main idea of this passage in a single sentence. Make it precise, concise, and memorable.

Spark Transformation

How does God's love move you to show love to others in your own life? Ask the Holy Spirit to show you who He wants to love through you today, and then make a specific plan for how you will love them in the next twenty-four hours.

Turn to God in Worship

Later in his epistle, the apostle John tells us that "God is love" (1 John 4:16), further expounding on the central truth that Jesus lived out love for all the world to see (1 John 3:16). According to the gospel of John 3:16–17, how did God show love toward the world? How did Jesus show love?

In what ways has God shown love to you specifically? Sing out some of your favorite praise songs and hymns about God's love today as an offering of praise to Him. (See some of my favorites in the *Bible and Breakfast* playlist available at bibleandbreakfast.com.)

What are some of your favorite hymns and praise songs about God's love? Share with us on social media using #bibleandbreakfast.

| **PREP TIME:** *10 minutes* | **COOK TIME:** *5 minutes* | **YIELD:** *4 servings* |

 Kid-friendly

————————

8 slices bacon (this is the "ham")

2 large avocados

4 slices sourdough bread

4 large eggs

Salt and pepper to taste

1. Cook bacon to desired crispiness. Set aside.

2. Mash avocados in a bowl and season with salt and pepper. Set aside.

3. Toast bread. Set aside. (See? You're so good at this!)

4. Fry your eggs to desired doneness. I like mine over easy.

5. Now it's time to assemble your breakfast! Slather avocado over your toast. Carefully slide egg in the center of the avocado toast. Top with two pieces of bacon in a crisscross pattern. Enjoy!

Avocado Toast with Bacon and Eggs

I was on my way to a Ladies' Christmas Brunch when I stopped by a local coffee shop for some coffee and breakfast. Their menu featured a variation on this dish and it had green eggs in the name, and I was intrigued enough to order it. (Although, is it really a good idea to order an unknown menu item before a big speaking engagement? Probably not. But what can I say—I like to live on the wild side.) I was delighted by their take on this Dr. Seuss classic: the green comes from mashed-up avocado spread on sour dough bread, and the egg was NOT green—it was a delicious over easy fried egg with a sprinkling of pepper and thinly sliced ham. I recreated the recipe here.

DAY 28
Indulging

 Snack on the go | *If you're in a rush, the short devotional below is a quick "spiritual snack" to feed your soul and meditate on all day long.*

Self-control.

What comes to mind when you hear that word? List a few of them in the space below:

Honestly, that word makes me cringe. I immediately think of a dozen areas I could be more self-controlled: my diet, my social media use, my bedtime routine, my temper, and my workouts, just to name a few.

Your areas of struggle may be different, but most of us could use more self-control. Even Solomon said: "Like a city whose walls are broken through is a person who lacks self-control" (Prov. 25:28).

That verse is worth both circling AND highlighting in your Bible. In Solomon's time, cities were only as safe as their walls were strong. A city with broken walls was vulnerable to enemy attack and occupation.

It is the same with our souls; the enemy is out to destroy us. He will use shady tactics to kill our hope and ruin our testimony, and sadly, he often finds an "in" through our self-indulgences.[19] Yes, those good gifts that comfort us can easily become the very things that threaten our spiritual vitality.

But before we despair, let's remember that self-control is the work of God's Spirit in us (Gal. 5:22–23). As we spend time in Jesus' presence, He transforms the desires of our hearts and empowers us to resist temptation. God is our refuge; He is our strength (Ps. 46:1). We can run to Him in time of trouble, because:

"No temptation has overtaken you except what is common to mankind. And God is faithful; he will not let you be tempted beyond what you can bear. But when you are tempted, he will also provide a way out so that you can endure it" (1 Cor. 10:13).

Did you get that? When temptation comes with its ramming horn busting against your walls of self-control, don't try to resist on your own. Run to Jesus, and ask for His supernatural strength to find the way out.

Feast at the table

If you have more time to linger at the breakfast table, open your Bible and let's FEAST on God's Word together!

Instead of focusing on just one topic, today I'm guiding you through a topical study on the word "self-control." This is our chance to put into practice all the Bible study skills we've learned so far. You can do this!

Focus on God

Open your Bible to Matthew 13:22–23 and ask God's Spirit to search your heart and reveal anything in your life that He wants to change as you study Scripture today.

Engage the Text

Do a search on self-control in the Bible. You can simply type "self-control Bible verses" into a search engine, or use the search tools on a site like BlueLetterBible.com.

Skim the passages listed, and then pick one passage to focus on. Read the passage out loud, and then write the verse(s) in the space below.

Now let's use the methods we've learned throughout this book to engage the text. Ask the journalistic questions (Who, What, When, Where, Why, and How) and write your answers. Feel free to chase rabbit trails, looking up cross-references and using a Bible dictionary to dig into the meaning of the word. Look for patterns in the text, or diagram the passage. Remember to ask yourself what this passage says about God and write down anything else that stands out to you.

For example, 2 Timothy 1:7 says: "For the Spirit God gave us does not make us timid, but gives us power, love and self-discipline." From this verse, I can learn that self-discipline comes from God's Spirit, and that He freely gives it to us. It also contrasts timidity with self-discipline. I wonder how fear affects my indulgences. And how do power, love, and self-discipline all go together in the area I struggle with most?

Assess the Main Idea

Write down the main idea of this passage in a single sentence that's easy for you to remember.

Spark Transformation

Ask the Holy Spirit to help you apply the main idea to your life. Where do you need His help to be more self-controlled? What would your life look like if you exhibited more self-control in this area?

Close your eyes and imagine that each time you resist, you are adding another brick to the wall of self-control that protects you. Those self-indulgences will grow less and less tempting with each victory.

Write a short prayer thanking God for the victories you've already experienced in your specific struggles. Ask Him to help you recognize the way out, and to strengthen you to resist temptation so you can practice self-control. Finally, proclaim His victory now, before you encounter temptation, so that when it comes, you will be reminded that He has already won the battle.

Turn to God in Worship

As I mentioned in today's "Snack on the Go," self-control is the fruit of the Spirit. Take time today to praise God for being all-powerful and for loving us enough to powerfully work in us.

Share your Spark Transformation application on social media using #bibleandbreakfast to keep you accountable!

❄ *Freezer-friendly*

⊘ *Gluten-free*

✋ *Kid-friendly*

☑ *Meal Prep*

2 cups blueberries

2 cups peeled and chopped peaches

1 tsp lemon juice

1 cup rolled oats

½ cup pecans or walnuts, chopped

½ cup almond meal

¼ cup maple syrup

¼ cup coconut oil, melted

½ tsp sea salt

½ tsp cinnamon

Whipped cream, for serving

1. Line a baking sheet with aluminum foil and place in the oven. (This will save you cleanup headaches later.) Preheat oven to 350° F.

2. Mix together the fruit and lemon juice in an 8x8 pan.

3. In a small bowl, stir together the rest of the ingredients. Spread over the fruit.

4. Place the 8x8 pan on the baking sheet in the oven. Bake until golden and bubbling, about 35 to 40 minutes. If you've pulled this from the freezer and you're baking it frozen (because you planned ahead and doubled the recipe last time, you wise woman!), you will need to bake it about 10 minutes longer.

5. Serve warm with freshly whipped cream or cold with a dollop of Greek yogurt. You can't go wrong either way. Yum!

Peach and Blueberry Crisp

Okay, so this is kind of like eating dessert for breakfast, but it's loaded with fruit and oats and nuts, so it's totally okay. Right? That's what I tell myself when I dig in, anyway. I usually make this in the evening for a light dessert after dinner and eat leftovers with Greek yogurt for breakfast. You can use any fruit you like, but peaches and blueberries are our family favorite, and the color combo makes me happy. You can even use frozen fruit if you bake for a bit longer (see note in step 4).

DAY 29
Pour Out

 *Snack on the go*

If you're in a rush, the short devotional below is a quick "spiritual snack" to feed your soul and meditate on all day long.

I sat in the college chapel service, tears streaming down my cheeks as the speaker recited the lyrics to a simple children's song: "My God is so big, so strong, and so mighty, there's nothing my God cannot do."[20]

I had sung that song many times, but the lyrics took on new meaning as the speaker whispered them again and again, challenging the room filled with thousands of college students to believe from the depths of our hearts.

Just that week, I had learned my parents were separating. After a lifetime of missionary work, my family was falling apart. And it felt like my world was crumbling around me.

Something broke inside too, as the tears flowed freely.

Did I really believe God was so big? So strong? So mighty?

Was He really so loving? So good? So kind?

Although that was years ago, I remember the heartbreak and uncertainty as if it was yesterday. Yet at that chapel service, two truths became my anchor throughout the tumultuous season to follow: God is all-powerful, and God is all-loving.

If God was loving but not powerful, He would be compassionate but unable to help us.

If God was powerful but not loving, He could help us but could also choose to ignore us.

But because God is both, He longs to rescue us and does so at great cost to Himself: He sent His own Son to bring us back into a relationship with Himself. And He continues to pour out His power and mercy to save us time and time again, even when the end result doesn't look like the fairy-tale ending we had envisioned.

We can join with David to say:

> *But I will sing of your strength,*
> *in the morning I will sing of your love;*
> *for you are my fortress,*
> *my refuge in times of trouble.*
>
> *You are my strength, I sing praise to you;*
> *you, God, are my fortress,*
> *my God on whom I can rely.* (Ps. 59:16–17)

In what area of your life do you need to trust God's love? His power? Write a prayer below, placing that situation into His care, declaring your trust in Him alone.

 **Feast at the table** | *If you have more time to linger at the breakfast table, open your Bible and let's FEAST on God's Word together!*

Focus on God

Open your Bible to Exodus 34:28 and ask the Lord to give you a greater hunger and thirst for His Word today.

Engage the Text

Read Psalm 59 out loud. You know the drill . . . read it again, slower this time, using your pencil to circle words or phrases that stand out. Write down your observations.

Read the superscription (the words before verse 1), and write what you learn about the circumstances surrounding this psalm.

If you're using a study Bible, you may notice a cross-reference to 1 Samuel 19. Turn there and read that chapter to understand the context. In one or two sentences, summarize what happened to cause David to cry out to God.

Psalm 59 was likely written during the circumstances described in 1 Samuel 19:11. What does this psalm say about the way David responded to life-threatening events?

What do we learn about how David handled fear in Psalm 59?

How did he grapple with uncertainty in his future?

What titles does David use to refer to God in this prayer? What does each title say about God's character?

What do verses 9 and 16 say about the state of David's heart during this tumultuous time in his life?

What attributes of God does David find comfort in during this time (see verses 16–17 especially)?

Was God faithful to protect David? Review 1 Samuel 19:18–24 and describe God's deliverance.

Assess the Main Idea

What do this story and the psalm together say about God's faithfulness in the midst of David's difficult circumstances? Write out the main idea, making it precise, concise, and memorable.

Spark Transformation

What is going on in your life right now that makes you want to run and hide? Read through Psalm 59 once more, this time personalizing it to your situation in life. What would it look like for you to trust God in this situation as David did in his?

Turn to God in Worship

The first half of this psalm is predominantly a prayer of desperation and the second half is predominantly an assurance of God's deliverance. As you pray this psalm to God, bow down to Him in worship, entrusting your life and all the details of your circumstances to Him, and declaring your trust in His deliverance.

❄ *Freezer-friendly*

✋ *Kid-friendly*

☑ *Meal Prep*

⊘ *Gluten-free*

6 Russet potatoes

8 large eggs

2 Tbsp butter

2 cups sour cream

Salt and pepper to taste

Optional add-ins: cooked kielbasa, cooked bacon, chopped onion or bell pepper, shredded Colby-Jack cheese

Parsley, optional

1. Preheat oven to 350° F.

2. Boil potatoes for 15 minutes and eggs for 10 minutes. Cool and peel. You can either slice the potatoes and eggs or grate them using a food processor with a grater attachment. Mix gently to avoid smashing.

3. In a small saucepan, stir butter and sour cream over low heat until melted. Remove from heat.

4. In a greased 9x13 casserole dish, layer half the grated potatoes and egg mixture, sprinkle with salt and pepper, and top with half the creamy sauce. Repeat, ending with a smooth layer of the sour cream mixture. (To meal prep, prepare through step 4, and then cover with plastic wrap and refrigerate up to 2 days in advance. When ready to bake, remove plastic wrap and bake an additional 5–10 minutes.)

5. Bake until golden brown on top, about 30 minutes. Serve warm with a sprinkling of parsley for color.

Easter Egg Potato Casserole

Every Easter, children around the world dye eggs and mothers around the world rack their brains to figure out what to do with all those extra eggs. This Romanian dish was a staple breakfast in the days following Easter when I was a child, and I was delighted by the flecks of pinks, blues, and greens that inevitably tinged our leftover Easter eggs. But you don't have to wait for Easter to enjoy this delicious breakfast casserole.

DAY 30
Morning . . . and Evening

 Snack on the go

Do you ever wonder what to pray? For years I'd wake up dutifully asking God to be with me and go to sleep thanking Him for His theoretical presence. But as I matured, I longed for more substantial prayers.

Then, a few years ago, a dear friend explained how she prays following the model of Psalm 92:1–2:

> It is good to praise the LORD
>   and make music to your name, O Most High,
> proclaiming your love in the morning
>   and your faithfulness at night.

My friend pointed out that the psalmist proclaimed *God's love* in the morning. The original Hebrew implies not just the feeling of love but the reality of God's promise-keeping nature, His *chesed*. When we proclaim God's love in the morning, we greet each day's uncertainties with bold declarations of God's unchanging character.[21]

Before our toes touch the ground, before our thumbs scroll the news, before we're overwhelmed with our to-dos, let us boldly declare God's lovingkindness. *Yes, even today, God is love. He is good. And He will keep His promises.* With this mindset, we can face whatever the day brings our way, because we've preemptively placed our trust in our loving God.

And as we pull the covers to our chins at night, we reflect on the day's events: *yes, even today, God was faithful. He was true to His character. He kept His Word.*

When the kids spilled glitter over the freshly mopped floors, God's presence soothed me. When the girls' night didn't include me, God was with me. When my coworker gossiped about me, God's love surrounded me.

This changes everything. We wake up reminding ourselves of who God is and we go to sleep recalling how He proved His character once again in the gritty details of everyday life. And in this simple practice, we're learning to see God's presence and to savor His goodness in our daily lives.

As you finish your *Bible and Breakfast* time today, pause to declare God's love over your life: *This is who He is.* And as you go to sleep tonight, reflect how He has been faithful to His promises in the day's events, and join with the psalmist in thanking Him.

 Feast at the table | *If you have more time to linger at the breakfast table, open your Bible and let's FEAST on God's Word together!*

Focus on God

Open your Bible to Matthew 24:35 and ask the Lord to awaken you to His surpassing beauty in Scripture and to stir in you a deeper longing for Him as you study it.

Engage the Text

Read Psalm 92 out loud. Read verses 1–2 again, slowly, focusing on each word as you speak it out loud.

Write it out in the space below.

What stands out to you in these verses?

Underline the three verbs used in these two verses. How is each action similar, and how is each unique?

According to this text, when is a good time to praise God?

What does the psalmist proclaim in the morning? What does he proclaim at night?

How does verse 4 add to our understanding of the psalmist's praise in verse 2?

The concept of lovingkindness is common in the Old Testament to describe God's covenantal love toward His people. Use a Bible dictionary to look up the meaning of this word, and write your observations below.

Now look up the word translated as "faithfulness" and write what you learn about it.

How are these two words similar? How are they different?

What two titles does the psalmist use to describe God in verse 1? What is the significance of God's name? Check the cross-references for this verse, and list what you learn about the Hebrew understanding of God's name.

This psalm begins with the phrase "it is good" and then goes on to list these acts of praise and worship. Based on what you learned in your study today, why are these activities good?

Assess the Main Idea

Write out the main idea of this passage in a single sentence. Make it precise, concise, and memorable.

Spark Transformation

This week, make it a practice to praise God for His love as soon as you wake up. Thank God that regardless what the day holds, He will still love you and be faithful to His promises to you. Praise Him for overseeing the day's activities and for His sustaining love that will carry you through the good and the bad moments. Then when you lie in bed at night, reflect on the day's events and praise God for His faithfulness—for the many ways He was present in your life, protected and provided for you, and pulled you close to His heart.

Turn to God in Worship

In Old Testament times, the names of God were considered a manifestation of His character. So to "make music to [God's] name" meant to praise God for all of His characteristics. In what ways has God revealed His characteristics in your life recently?

Praise Him for His name in your life. You may even want to worship Him from A–Z, listing a different attribute or name for each letter of the alphabet.

Don't forget to tag me @asheritah on social media to share what you've learned this week in your Bible and Breakfast time. I want to hear from you!

⊘ *Gluten-free*

✋ *Kid-friendly*

☑ *Meal Prep*

---

3 large bananas

¼ cup coconut oil, melted

1 tsp vanilla extract

2 cups rolled oats

⅔ cup almond flour

⅓ cup unsweetened coconut flakes

⅓ cup toasted walnuts, chopped

⅓ cup dried cranberries

⅓ cup mini chocolate chips

1 tsp baking powder

¼ tsp sea salt

Extra nuts and chocolate chips for
   topping

1. Preheat oven to 350° F. (To save time, toast the walnuts on a baking sheet while the oven preheats. Stir occasionally.)

2. In a large bowl, mash the bananas with a fork until smooth. Stir in coconut oil and vanilla.

3. Mix in the rest of the ingredients until just combined. The dough will seem looser than your typical cookie dough, but that's okay.

4. Drop heaping tablespoons of dough onto a baking sheet, about an inch apart. These cookies won't spread during baking, so flatten them with the back of a fork. Sprinkle extra walnuts and chocolate chips on top and gently press them into the dough.

5. Bake for 14–16 minutes. Remove from oven and let cool for a few minutes, and then transfer to a wire rack to cool completely. Or eat one while it's warm and the chocolate is still gooey. I won't judge. In fact, I would probably be eating a warm one right there with you. Enjoy!

Banana Nut Cookies

Here we go! We're wrapping up this recipe collection with cookies for breakfast. Yes, please! (But *Bible and Breakfast* doesn't end here, of course. Read on to Day 31 and "Where do we go from here?" to continue your daily habit!)

DAY 31
Breaking Bread Together

 Snack on the go

If you're in a rush, the short devotional below is a quick "spiritual snack" to feed your soul and meditate on all day long.

As a child, I watched my parents welcome hundreds of people into our home. A massive walnut table took up most of our living space, and though it was meant to seat eight, many more crammed around for a bite of my mom's delicious cooking.

Now that I'm an adult, I realize all the work that goes into extending hospitality: meal planning and grocery shopping, chopping (oh SO MUCH chopping), sautéing, cleaning. And somehow it seems we never have enough chairs to seat everyone around the table.

But you know what? I've found that people don't care so much about elbow room as they do about finding a safe space to know and be known.[22]

I'm reminded of this truth every time I look up to read the large farmhouse sign above our table: "They broke bread in their homes and ate together with glad and sincere hearts" (Acts 2:46b).

No pretense of perfection. No fake smiles. Just glad and sincere hearts.

If you come to my home, you'll likely see crumbs under the table and watercolor smears on the wood. With three kids five and under, my home is never sparkling clean, but I hope it radiates warmth. I want my children to witness friendships forged over casseroles and belly laughs over brownies, life-changing discipleship one meal at a time.

This is the heart of hospitality, and this is where *Bible and Breakfast* melds into a beautiful expression of love. First we experience Jesus' hospitality as He invites us to spend our mornings with Him, and then we extend that invitation to someone else to join us in our new habit.

Who is one person you've been meaning to invite over to your house? Write their name below, and then write a short prayer asking the Lord to give you courage to open the door.

Now pick up your phone and invite them to come over. Make a simple breakfast, and share one thing you've learned in your *Bible and Breakfast* time with Jesus these last 31 days. Ask her to join you in reading His Word together, and grow together in your love for Jesus and for one another. Share laughter and burdens as you wipe the coffee rings from this book, and let this become a written journal of your encounters with Jesus together over the next 31 days.

Feast at the table

If you have more time to linger at the breakfast table, open your Bible and let's FEAST on God's Word together!

Focus on God

Open your Bible to read John 15:7, turning it into a prayer as you begin today's study.

Engage the Text

Read Acts 2:42–47 out loud. Read it again, writing down your observations.

According to verse 41, who's the "they" referred to in verse 42?

What were the essential things they did together?

What is the significance of these four disciplines in the life of the early church?

Look up the cross-references for one of the four activities. What do these other passages add to your understanding of that discipline?

What else did this group of Christians do, according to verses 44–45?

How did the surrounding people react to this group of Christians, according to the text?

What other activities did the early church practice in their homes, according to verse 46?

What is the general tone in this passage? In other words, what's the predominant mood of believers here?

Look up the word "devoted" in the original Greek. What is the significance of this word in the life of the believer?

What do you learn about the character of God from this passage?

Assess the Main Idea

Write out the main idea of this passage in a single sentence. Make it precise, concise, and memorable.

Spark Transformation

First-century Christians in Jerusalem were devoted. What does that devotion look like in your life? Which of the four disciplines comes easiest to you? Which is hardest? Ask the Holy Spirit to show you how to devote yourself to Him and how to continue growing spiritually as you journey with Him.

Turn to God in Worship

As we conclude this *Bible and Breakfast* challenge, worship God for His goodness in providing ways for us to grow spiritually, to know Him better, and to fellowship with other believers. Then ask Him to continue growing you in your daily habit of meeting with Jesus over breakfast, and inviting others to join you.

Where do we go from here?

Well, you did it! You finished the 31-day challenge of *Bible and Breakfast*, enjoying time with Jesus every morning whether through small "Snacks" at a time or FEASTing on the texts or a little of both. Way to go!

Reaching the end of a Bible study is both exciting and a bit disorienting, isn't it? You might be wondering, "Where do I go from here?"

First of all, I encourage you to take a few minutes to reflect on your Bible study experience these last 31 days. What have you learned about Jesus? How have you grown in your love and knowledge of Him? (Journal your thoughts below.)

What did you learn about yourself?

What did you enjoy most about your *Bible and Breakfast* habit?

What tweaks can you make to your morning time with Jesus to create a stronger and more enjoyable habit?

What would you like to say to Jesus as you reflect on the past weeks together? In the space below, write a few words of worship, praise, gratitude, or rededication.

Have you grown in your love for Jesus and His Word over the last month? Friend, that's fantastic news! It means His Holy Spirit is stirring in you a hunger and desire for Him, and He promises to satisfy that hunger with more of Himself (Matt. 5:6). Continue your daily *Bible and Breakfast* habit and watch as He continues drawing you closer to Himself (James 4:8).

Next, connect with others in your local church, and look for ways to serve and continue to grow in community. You can find more studies and devotionals for individual and group use at asheritah.com, including my 6-week study of Colossians, *He Is Enough: Living in the Fullness of Jesus*.

Lastly, I would love for you to share *Bible and Breakfast* with a few of your friends. If you grew closer to Jesus over the last few weeks, wouldn't they want that too? What would it look like to invite another person into that experience with you?

Maybe you could bring together a group of women to go through this book together, meeting once a week to share insights into Scripture over your favorite breakfast recipe that week. Consider starting a cooking club with a few of your neighbors, trying out new recipes while also talking about your journey with Jesus. Perhaps you could invite a few high school girls into your home and teach them some cooking basics while journeying through this book together. Or maybe you can invite friends around the country to join you in a private Facebook group or via text message to study together. The possibilities are endless!

Whatever your next steps look like, I pray you will continue to meet with Jesus over breakfast and develop new spiritual habits throughout your day. I wish we could have cooked all these recipes together, but someday, we will join together in the marriage supper of the Lamb. And oh, what a glorious meal that will be, eating and drinking together with the Bread and Water of Life!

The Spirit and the bride say, "Come!"
And let the one who hears say, "Come!"
Let the one who is thirsty come;
and let the one who wishes
take the free gift of the water of life.
(Rev. 22:17)

With much joy,

Asheritah

You've likely learned a few things about spending time
with Jesus in the mornings. I encourage you to continue
this habit into the coming months, and consider adding
another tiny Quiet Time habit to your day.
For more ideas and a Quiet Time Guide, go to

bibleandbreakfast.com

Recipe Index by Tags

Acknowledgments

To my onethingalone.com blog readers, especially those who joined me in the original *Bible and Breakfast*, thank you! Your companionship during those first 31 days kept me going, and your emails over the past few years convinced me that this blog series could be a book. I couldn't have done this without you.

I'm indebted to the incredible women who contributed to the original "31 days of Bible and Breakfast" blog series in October 2016. There's nothing like peer pressure to get you to stick to outlandish goals, and these ladies kept me writing for 31 days straight, which led to the book you're holding in your hands. These women continue to inspire me to grow closer to Jesus and use digital tools to build His kingdom. (Curious who these mysterious writers are? Go to bibleandbreakfast.com to find a complete listing of their names and websites.)

Tawny, your wise counsel was again invaluable. Judy, you believed in this project before I really did. Amanda, the pages bled red and this book is the better for it. Erik, as always your eye for design turned this into the gorgeous book it is. Ashley T., you tirelessly championed this project to get it into the hands of women who need it. Janis, Grace, Adam, Richard, Randall, and the entire Moody Publishers team—I couldn't ask for better partners in writing and publishing. Thank you. It's an honor to co-labor with you all.

Ashley M., you radiate joy wherever you go. I was thrilled when you joined this project! Thank you for praying me through the toughest days and capturing such tender moments. You're a rare gift, friend.

Carmen and Wendy, every writer needs prayer warriors like you by their side. Thank you for upholding me when I grew weak, for reminding me of truths when I doubted, and for speaking life over me and my family. Jennifer, thank you for teaching me how to pray Psalm 92 and for changing my life with your quiche. I'm a more powerful prayer warrior because of you.

Mom, I love cooking because of you. From sautéing mushrooms to making homemade béchamel sauce, you've taught me how to turn simple ingredients into delicious meals, and it's a joy to watch you teach my children the same.

Carissa, Amelia, and Theo, thank you for bringing my Bible to the table on the days I forget, and for bringing narratives to life with your childlike faith. I've learned more about Jesus by reading the gospels with you than I have in hundreds of Sunday morning sermons. Being your mom is a treasured joy.

Flaviu, while I wrote a book on Bible and breakfast, you fed our family and cared for our most basic needs. Even though my name is on this cover, yours belongs right next to it. I couldn't do what I do without you. Thank you, darling.

Beloved Jesus, there would be no *Bible and Breakfast* were it not for You. I picture the grilled fish you prepared for Your disciples on the beach that morning so long ago,[23] and I wish I would have been there too. And yet, You graciously invite me to breakfast with You each and every morning. Thank You. I can't wait to break bread with You in person soon.

Notes

1. The 2016 Barna survey revealed that 61% of Americans want to read the Bible more (women were more likely to express this desire than men, 68% of women compared to 54% of men). But over the previous 12 months, only 23% of those surveyed said their Bible use increased, while 8% said their Bible use actually decreased. The top reason for lower Bible engagement (58%) was that respondents felt too busy with life's responsibilities, which—let's face it—is what plagues most of us, right?

2. "Bible Reading in 2017: A New Year's Resolution." Barna Group, January 18, 2017, www.barna.com/research/bible-reading-2017-new-years-resolution.

3. See John 4:4–26.

4. See Matthew 9:20–22.

5. See Luke 10:38–42.

6. A 2017 study from Lifeway Research found that the biggest factor that influenced young adults' spiritual health was regular Bible reading. This ought not to discourage us or heap guilt on us, but rather encourage us to persevere through the inconveniences of reading the Bible with our kids, knowing that those moments add up to significant life change. See "Young Bible Readers More Likely to be Faithful Adults, Study Finds," LifeWay Research, October 17, 2017, https://lifewayresearch.com/2017/10/17/young-bible-readers-more-likely-to-be-faithful-adults-study-finds.

7. A few months prior to preparing this book for publication, I read *Together: Growing Appetites for God* by Carrie Ward (Chicago: Moody, 2012), and was encouraged by her adventures in reading through the whole Bible multiple times with her little crew. Her story deeply affected me, especially after meeting one of her sons and seeing on his face the light of God's presence—imprinted on his soul, I'm sure, through the thousands of mornings spent listening to God's Word around the breakfast table. I've been emboldened to welcome my children into my Bible reading habit, even if it's louder, messier, and harder than reading on my own, and it's been a game-changer for all of us. Go to www.bibleandbreakfast.com to find some of my favorite practical tips when reading the Bible with kids.

8. Leticia Ramírez-Lugo, et al, "Choice Behavior Guided by Learned, But Not Innate, Taste Aversion Recruits the Orbitofrontal Cortex," *Journal of Neuroscience*, Society for Neuroscience (Oct. 12, 2016): www.jneurosci.org/content/36/41/10574.

9. A fantastic read on this topic is the little book *50 Reasons Why Jesus Came to Die* by John Piper (Carol Stream, IL: Crossway, 2006).

10. "Music Changes Perception, Research Shows," University of Groningen, ScienceDaily, April 27, 2011, https://www.sciencedaily.com/releases/2011/04/110427101606.htm.

11. Samuel Medley, "The Wisdom and Goodness of God," in William Gadsby, *A Selection of Hymns for Public Worship. In Four Parts* (Manchester: J. Gadsby; London: R. Groombridge, 1844), hymn 7.

12. This popular quote is a paraphrase of a quote from the sermon in which Charles Spurgeon also references the preceding hymn lyrics: C. H. Spurgeon, "A Happy Christian," *Spurgeon's Sermons* Volume 13, No. 736 (1867), https://www.ccel.org/ccel/spurgeon/sermons13.ix.html.

13. For more on this topic, read my upcoming book *Uncovering the Love of Jesus: A Lent Devotional* (Chicago: Moody, 2020).

14. Find more information about this annual event in Wendy Speake's book *The 40-Day Sugar Fast: Where Physical Detox Meets Spiritual Transformation* (Grand Rapids, MI: Baker, 2019).

15. "The Westminster Shorter Catechism," *The Westminster Presbyterian*, http://www.westminsterconfession.org/confessional-standards/the-westminster-shorter-catechism.php.

16. John Piper, *Desiring God: Meditations of a Christian Hedonist* (Colorado Springs: Multnomah, 1986), 309.

17. Thomas J. Herbert, "Form and Photosynthesis in Vascular Plants," *Arrangement of Leaves and Heliotropism* (2004): www.bio.miami.edu/tom/courses/bil160/bil160goods/plantform/13_plantform.html.

18. For a deeper study of contentment, spiritual blessings, and the sufficiency and supremacy of Jesus, pick up my 6-week study of Colossians titled *He Is Enough: Living in the Fullness of Jesus* (Chicago: Moody, 2018).

19. I write extensively on our enemy's tactics to cripple us in these spiritual battles in chapters 1–3 of *Full: Food, Jesus, and the Battle for Satisfaction* (Chicago: Moody, 2017). In the years since its release, I've heard from thousands of readers who now have renewed hope and have begun rebuilding the wall of self-control by applying the practical principles outlined in those chapters. Others who don't struggle with food fixation have also applied these principles to other areas of their lives with great success too. If you're struggling with self-control, consider picking up a copy of *Full* to read for yourself.

20. Ruth Harms Calkin, "My God Is So Big," copyright © 1960, 2002.

21. In order for us to declare who God is, we must know Him. I've found it particularly helpful to study His names and how they reflect His character, and I've shared my findings in my book *Unwrapping the Names of Jesus* (Chicago: Moody, 2017). Yes, it's an Advent devotional, but honestly this practice is helpful all year round.

22. I didn't realize how many insecurities I had about opening my home to others until I read *Just Open the Door* (Nashville: B&H Books, 2018) by my friend Jen Schmidt. Beautifully written with heartfelt encouragement and practical advice, this book gave me the gentle nudge I needed to practice imperfect hospitality. The emphasis on using *Bible and Breakfast* to reach out and invite others into our homes comes as much from my childhood experience as it does from this book's influence.

23. For this fascinating story, read John 21:1–14.

ONE THING ALONE
MINISTRIES

We help women enjoy time with Jesus every day

Discover simple ways to find joy in Jesus through creative and consistent time in His Word.

Start Today
onethingalone.com

Discover the Secret to a Full Life

978-0-8024-1686-5

In this 6-week study of Colossians, Asheritah Ciuciu leads readers to discover the life-altering importance of Jesus' sufficiency and sovereignty. With short meditations for busy days, dig-deep study for days you want more, and supplemental service challenges for leaders, you can study the way that helps you the most.

Also available as an eBook

MOODY Publishers®

From the Word *to Life*®

Can the Bible help me with my food struggles?

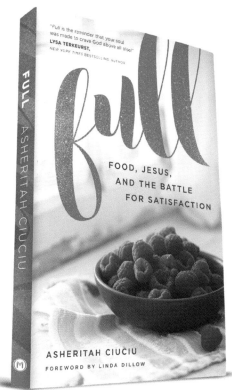

978-0-8024-1537-0

Whether the struggle is with excess weight, unwanted cravings, total control, or extreme diets, we all have a relationship with food. *Full* unpacks a theology of food to break its power, help us engage food holistically, and free us to taste and see that God is good.

Also available as an eBook

MOODY
Publishers

*From the Word **to** Life*

Seasonal Devotionals from Asheritah Ciuciu

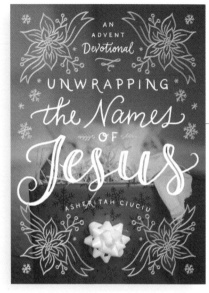

978-0-8024-1672-8

Unwrapping the Names of Jesus leads readers through the four weeks of Advent (Hope, Preparation, Joy, and Love) by focusing each day's reflection on one name of Jesus. Each week begins with an interactive family devotional followed by five daily reflections, as well as suggestions for fun-filled family activities or service projects to enhance a family's Advent experience.

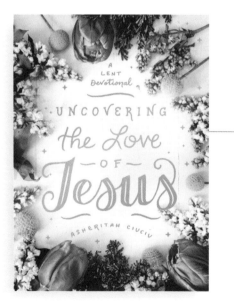

978-0-8024-1949-1

Uncovering the Love of Jesus takes you through the 40 days of Lent and helps you prepare for Easter by focusing your attention on the One at the center of it all: Jesus. Each week begins with an interactive Lent Celebration that can include the whole family. This is followed by five daily reflections on a story from Jesus' life and ministry that reveals a different aspect of His love. At the end of the week, you'll find activity ideas and challenges that help you live out the love of Jesus.

Also available as eBooks

MOODY
Publishers®

From the Word to Life®